33

$\frac{3600}{80€}$

LABOUR
AND
BUSINESS
IN
MODERN BRITAIN

edited by
Charles Harvey
and
John Turner

FRANK CASS

First published in 1989 in Great Britain by
FRANK CASS AND COMPANY LIMITED
Gainsborough House, 11 Gainsborough Road,
London E11 1RS

and in the United States of America by
FRANK CASS
c/o Biblio Distribution Center
8705 Bollman Place
Savage, MD 20763

British Library Cataloguing in Publication Data

Labour and business in modern Britain
  1. Great Britain. Industrial relations.
  History
  I. Turner, John, *1949–*
  II. Harvey, Charles, *1950–*
  III. Business history, ISSN 0007–6791
  331′.0941

    ISBN 0–7146–3365–8

Library of Congress Cataloging-in-Publication Data

Labour and business in modern Britain / edited by Charles Harvey and
  John Turner.
      p.   cm.
      "This group of studies first appeared in a special issue on labour
  and business in modern Britain, Business history, vol. xxxi, no. 2"-
  -T.p. verso.
      Includes index.
      ISBN 0–7146–3365–8
      1. Industrial relations—Great Britain—History.   I. Harvey,
  Charles, 1950–   . II. Turner, John, 1949 May 18-
  HD8388.L34 1989   89–7050
  331′.0941—dc19   CIP

This group of studies first appeared in a Special Issue on
Labour and Business in Modern Britain, *Business History*, Vol.XXXI, No.2 (April 1989).

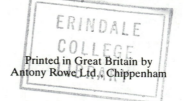

Printed in Great Britain by
Antony Rowe Ltd., Chippenham

CONTENTS

LABOUR AND BUSINESS IN MODERN BRITAIN

By JOHN TURNER

When business history was company history, the history of relations with employees played a larger or smaller part in the writing of business history according to the interests of company historians. In most of the better, and therefore classic accounts of British companies, there is a chapter or two on the recruitment and payment of the company's work-force, often accompanied by an account of the management's attitude towards trade unions. There it has tended to rest, until a nagging sense of guilt about the importance of comparative and theoretical studies of business activity began to infect the discipline, with results that can now be seen in the pages of *Business History* and other journals. Historians whose commitment to abstraction extended no further than the eco-nomic insight of all sensible men were suddenly confronted with the pains and pleasures of anthropology, sociology and even theoretical micro-economics. Inevitably the study of the workforce, both as a factor of production and as an element in the complex social structure we call 'the firm', has grown in sophistication, and no less inevitably business historians have been made aware of the huge scholarly industry of 'industrial relations'. Over much the same period the historiography of industrial relations has itself been transformed. Just as business history has developed beyond company history, industrial relations history has broken away from the history of trade unions and begun to embrace comparative studies, functional analyses of organisation and strike activity, occupational psychology, and most importantly the study of the 'labour process' and the dynamics of the labour market.

The articles in this volume, restricted, but only for convenience, to the history of industrial relations in British business, exemplify the important empirical research which is now possible because of the conceptual advances in business and industrial relations history in the last fifteen years. Each stands alone as an investigation of an important episode, an important industry, or an important theoretical question refracted through an historical problem. Nevertheless, they are all part of an intellectual process whereby business history and industrial relations history are moving forward together to provide a more convincing and lifelike interpretation of the industrial past in all developed countries. The purpose of this introduction is to outline the intellectual context in which they have been written.

Interpretations of industrial society are as old as industrial society itself. Every historian of 'organised business' knows by heart Adam Smith's observation that 'people of the same trade seldom meet together, even for merriment and diversion, but the conversation ends in a conspiracy against the public, or in some contrivance to raise prices', and Howard Gospel quotes in his article below the corollary: 'Masters are always and everywhere in a sort of tacit, but constant and uniform combination, not to raise the wages of labour above their actual rate'.[1] Smith's lucid analysis of the social dynamics of the industrialisation of Britain which he saw around him was far more critical of industrialisation's consequences than many of his intellectual opponents have allowed. But the most profound early critique of industrialisation undoubtedly came from Marx, who paradoxically developed his analysis of the division and alienation of labour in such a way that for many years the history of working-class politics was studied in isolation from the history of the labour process. Marx was heavily influenced in his study of factory labour by the work of Andrew Ure, whose *Factory Philosophy*, an account of the organisation of work in textile mills, helped to lead him to the notion that industrialisation reduced labour to a commodity. Marx's conceptual leap, to an economics based on a labour theory of value and a political prophecy of inevitable revolution, brought European social thought to adulthood by confronting it with an apocalyptic rendering of the potential consequences of economic change. The tricky question of what actually went on in the factories, workshops and sweatshops of industrial Britain was left behind and increasingly taken for granted by those who trod in his footsteps.

Other intellectual traditions conspired for many years to look past the organisations and experience of working life to the political and institutional forms which the labour movement adopted in the attempt to do something about them. Liberal students of late-nineteenth-century urban society penetrated the workman's home, fingered his household budget, cross-examined his common-law wife and pronounced on the degree of his individual responsibility for his manifest poverty. The New Liberalism of Hobson and Hobhouse found a structural link between his low wages and an 'underconsumptionist' explanation of Britain's comparatively low rate of economic growth. Sidney and Beatrice Webb, in their massive research for *Industrial Democracy* (1902) and *Problems of Modern Industry* (1902), interrogated workmen in large numbers about the process of work and the conflicts it caused, but continued to revise and re-issue their *History of Trade Unionism*, which placed the development of trade unions at the centre of industrial relations history. It is hardly surprising therefore that despite a huge body of available evidence on working conditions, much of it in print,[2] historians have found it attractive to explain the predicament of workers in terms of the economic contradictions of capitalism, and explain the workers' response as an ever more sophisticated effort to organise through trade unions and ultimately the Labour Party to defend class interests.

For a great deal of the twentieth century, therefore, the writing of industrial relations history has been dominated by institutional histories of trade unions and accounts of the 'system' of industrial relations in which the constituent parts were trade unions, employers' associations and, latterly, the government.[3] Even Marxist writers, isolated as they were from the mainstream, concentrated their efforts on the structure of trade unions.[4] One group of social historians who almost managed to avoid this narrowing of perspective were the intellectual heirs of Eric Hobsbawm, who in 1964 disinterred the 'Labour Aristocracy'.[5] This troublesome but self-sufficient group had been identified by Marx and Engels and re-examined by Lenin. Their responsibility for the quiescence of mid-Victorian Britain was suspected by all on the Left, and Hobsbawm attempted a definition which could form the basis of historical enquiry. He proposed that a working-class elite could be identified by its higher level of wages, its authority over other workers at work, and the degree of autonomy its members enjoyed in their work. Hobsbawm, and many writers who followed him, tended to emphasise wage differentials as the key to the difference between the Labour Aristocracy and other workers, since the other indicators varied very significantly from place to place and period to period. This caution, which in retrospect seems very important, led many historians to emphasise once more the life of the working class outside the workplace. Although a great deal of fascinating work has been done on working-class stratification and politics, the Marxist shyness of the workplace itself as a subject of study has been infectious.

In 1974 Harry Braverman, an American sociologist in the neo-Marxist tradition, published *Labour and Monopoly Capitalism,* which at last reinterpreted class struggle in terms of workplace experience and began a tradition of debate in which business historians would be able to participate. Braverman's interpretation was just as crudely schematic as Marx's original effort. He revised Marx's three stage model of industrialisation (co-operation, manufacture, machinofacture) by adding the development stage of 'monopoly capitalism'. This stage, characterised by the existence of large firms enjoying monopolistic or oligopolistic control of their product and labour markets, might be recognised by business historians as the Chandler thesis seen through a glass darkly: Chandler's emphasis on the tendency of growing companies to internalise decisions which in an earlier stage were left to the market is given a demonic twist in Braverman's description of the methods of labour-process control. Monopoly capitalist employers control their workforce by 'de-skilling', removing all decisions about work from the employee to a management team and forcing down wages by using labour-saving capital equipment and employing semi-skilled and unskilled labour instead of skilled artisans. Instead of Marx's Andrew Ure, Braverman chose Frederick Taylor as a writer on which to model his ideal type of a workplace under modern industrial capitalism, and his empirical evidence was drawn loosely from Ford's Detroit rather than from the textile mills. He assumed, and asserted, that modern employers adopted the 'scientific management' principles which Taylor had prescribed, and that the result was a new form of industrial serfdom.

Both business and industrial relations historians have had a protracted field day with Braverman. His insistence on a single line of evolution in management methods simply would not stand up to empirical enquiry, even for the United States. A broader perspective, which included the labour market theories described below, was introduced by Edwards, and an active empirical investigation of the labour process was begun.[6] Historians of industrial relations in the United Kingdom have shown that scientific management was resisted by employers as much as by workers; studies of the motor industry and other engineering industries have established that the rigid manufacturing patterns associated with Henry Ford never became effective in Britain. Students of company structure are even beginning to question the Chandlerian account of company growth, at least as it concerns Britain. Nevertheless, the questions Braverman and Edwards began to ask are being answered in rich detail.[7]

Two of the contributors to this volume, Howard Gospel and Jonathan Zeitlin, were early participants in the debate. Gospel's collection of essays, published with Craig Littler in 1983,[8] emphasised the degree to which employers' strategies helped to determine the nature of industrial relations. Gospel himself insisted that these strategies did not always conform either to Marxist or neo-Marxist models.[9] Zeitlin, in the same volume, explained how engineering employers were not forced to adopt new strategies by the conjunction of external economic pressures which, in Braverman's view, would have obliged them to shift towards monopoly capitalism; Wayne Lewchuk described and explained the many respects in which British car manufacture did not match the 'monopoly capitalist' stereotype.[10] That employers had not behaved as predicted led some historians to guess that workers would not have responded as predicted either, and the result of empirical research on shop-floor reactions, especially during the First World War, has led to a reappraisal of the effect of workplace struggles on the wider political situation. Alastair Reid questioned both the assumption that industrial change tended to weaken working class influence and the even more prevalent assumption that shopfloor responses to the extension of employer control were either based upon or likely to lead to revolutionary politics.[11]

Examination of employer strategies in the workplace leads logically on to examination of employer strategies for controlling the situation outside the workplace. This can, of course, involve political parties and the apparatus of the state as well as relations with employees, and this is beyond the scope of this volume.[12] Where employees are involved, historians have drawn on two further traditions of enquiry. One of these is the urban socio-political history exemplified by Patrick Joyce's *Work, Society and Politics*,[13] which dissects the society of northern mill-towns in the nineteenth century to explain how relations between paternalist employers and ostensibly deferential employees helped to determine the appearance of popular conservatism and a relatively stable non-revolutionary society in late-Victorian England. This amounted to a reinterpretation of the phenomenon which the labour aristocracy theory had purported to explain, with an emphasis on the behaviour of employers towards their workers. Another recently popular theme is the study of welfare policy as a device for control, both within the company unit and in the world outside. This was initiated by J.R. Hay, but more recently the work of Joseph Melling and Robert Fitzgerald has extended and broadened the enquiry. Fitzgerald in particular has used a Chandlerian model of company adaptation to market change to explain the parallel evolution of welfare provision.[14]

The final strand in recent scholarly work on business and labour is the systematic study of the labour market, drawing upon the model of a segmented labour market first proposed in abstract terms by Doeringer and Piore.[15] In brief, historians have proposed that the labour market was divided into a matrix whose dimensions were primary/secondary and internal/external, with comparatively little movement between them. Each segment had a distinctive pattern of action. The primary markets consisted of skilled and fairly affluent workers, compared with unskilled or semi-skilled and marginal workers in the secondary markets. External markets were labour markets of the neo-classical type, in which no actor had sufficient control to influence prices and wage rates were determined by supply and demand; internal markets were controlled by large employers, with jobs allocated to long-service workers. This abstraction has been particularly useful to historians trying to make sense of employers' and workers' attitudes to skill in the late nineteenth and twentieth centuries. Skilled workers in the nineteenth century were naturally in the primary labour market. Some, like time-served engineers, operated in an external market; others, like the highly-paid spinners whose political quiescence is noted by Joyce, can be seen as part of an internal market. Much of the turmoil in the labour process in the late Victorian period, which saw struggles between employers and skilled workers over the introduction both of machinery and new, more intrusive forms of management, can be interpreted as an attempt by employers to shift the emphasis from external to internal markets which they could more readily control. This corresponded to, and indeed supported, the effort to internalise product markets as well, as Gospel observes in his article in this volume.

Three themes therefore permeate the studies presented in this volume: the study of the labour process as an object of interest to employers and labour alike, the link between industrial relations policies and the role of the company in product and labour markets, and the use of diverse techniques, including welfare policy, to entrench employers' control over the labour market. The first essay, by Diane Drummond, builds on her pioneering work on the railway town of Crewe. It discusses the important interaction between factory power struggles and political developments outside, which Joyce adumbrated but did not fully develop, and also examines the adaptation of company labour strategy to the peculiar conditions of the industry and the time. This theme of contingency

– the power of small particularities to determine great outcomes – is taken up by McKinlay and Zeitlin, who reassess the experience of the engineering industry at the turn of the century and go on to question the functions of employers' associations. This is a question also addressed by Gospel, whose study of the flour-milling industry makes the most explicit use among the articles in this volume of the linkage between product and labour markets. The role of employers' associations as organisers of industrial relations policy, providing both leadership and services where companies themselves were unable to do so, has been a continuing theme in the history of organised business; Gospel's work reinforces the conclusion that increases in company size and improvements in company structure corresponding, but only roughly, to the Chandler model, were accompanied in Britain by a reduction in the importance of employers' associations and a matching growth in the importance of company labour policies.

Other articles stress the point that a company's labour strategies were constrained by the economic environment and by internal resources. Fitzgerald's study of Bryant and May extends his major work on the function of welfare policy with a fine-grained analysis of the instrumental role of welfare after the notorious Match Girls' Strike; but he also emphasises the limits placed on the development of a welfare-dominated labour market policy by the slow development of Bryant and May's management structure. Different handicaps afflicted different industries. The economic paralysis of the railways between the wars dictated the stasis in industrial relations which Crompton describes in his article. In the Coventry motor-car industry, neither the companies nor the trade unions had the organisational sophistication to develop a coherent bargaining system, and as the initiative drifted to the shop-floor the capacity of the firms to manage their own enterprises in a competitive environment was fatally sapped. Donnelly and Thoms make it clear that management weaknesses contributed to this outcome.

In all these studies it is clear that the history of industrial relations is at least as much part of business history as it is of 'labour history' or political history. What happened on the shop floor was determined by a process of bargaining ('struggle' in other terminology) between employers and workers. Employers' strategies were an integral part of their business strategies, and were constrained by many of the limitations, economic, psychological and human, which constrained their business development. Employers' strategies contributed as much as workers' strategies to the final outcome, and the strategies themselves were subject to a process of bargaining between the two sides of industry.[16] Labour as a factor of production is important to almost every business; and business's management of labour, an especially complex, unpredictable and varied resource, is one of the most important problems for any business historian to study.

Royal Holloway and Bedford New College, London

NOTES

1. Adam Smith, *An Inquiry into the Nature and Causes of the Wealth of Nations* (Cannan's edn., London, 1904), I, pp.130, 63.
2. Especially the proceedings of the Royal Commissions on Depression in Trade (1886), PP, 1886, XXIII and XXIII and the Royal Commission on Labour, PP, 1893–94, XXXII, leaving aside the huge contemporary literature in trade journals such as *Engineering*.
3. For a somewhat fuller discussion of this point see John Turner, 'Man and Braverman: British Industrial Relations', *History* (1986), pp.236–42.
4. For example, V.L. Allen, *Power in Trade Unions* (London, 1954).
5. In chapter 15 of *Labouring Men* (London, 1964). See also V.I. Lenin, *Imperialism, the Highest Stage of Capitalism* and K. Marx and F. Engels, *On Britain*.
7. See also Craig R. Littler, *The Development of the Labour Process in Capitalist Societies* (London, 1982).
6. R. Edwards, *Contested Terrain* (New York, 1979).
8. Howard Gospel and Craig Littler, *Managerial Strategies and Industrial Relations* (London, 1983).
9. Ibid., pp.1–24.
10. Ibid., pp.25–54, 82–110.
11. Alastair Reid, 'Dilution, trade unionism and the state in Britain during the First World War', in S. Tolliday and J. Zeitlin, *Shop Floor Bargaining and the State* (Cambridge, 1985); see also J.M. Hinton, *The First Shop Stewards' Movement* (London, 1973), countered by Ian McLean, *The Legend of Red Clydeside* (London, 1983).
12. For a sample of work on the other aspects, see John Turner (ed.), *Businessmen and Politics* (London, 1984).
13. Patrick Joyce, *Work, Society and Politics* (Brighton, 1980).
14. J.R. Hay, 'Employers and Social Policy in Britain: the Evolution of Welfare Legislation, 1905–14', *Social History*, Vol.2 (1977), pp.435–55; Robert Fitzgerald, *British Labour Management and Industrial Welfare* (London, 1988); Joseph Melling, 'British Employers and the Development of Industrial Welfare, c. 1880–1920' (University of Glasgow Ph.D. thesis, 1979); see also Derek Matthews, 'Profit-Sharing in the Gas Industry, 1889–1949', *Business History*, Vol.XXX, No.3 (1988), pp.306–28. There is a huge literature on 'welfare capitalism' in the United States, for example, S. Brandes, *American Welfare Capitalism, 1880–1940* (Cambridge, MA, 1976).
15. P.B. Doeringer and M.J. Piore, *Internal Labour Markets and Manpower Analysis* (New York, 1971).
16. Consequently the state was usually on the periphery of industrial relations, except in wartime, and this is properly reflected in the paucity of references to government in this collection.

'SPECIFICALLY DESIGNED'? EMPLOYERS' LABOUR STRATEGIES AND WORKER RESPONSES IN BRITISH RAILWAY WORKSHOPS, 1838–1914

By DI DRUMMOND

In a recent essay Eric Hobsbawm observes that 'the labour policies of the railway companies sometimes look as though they had been specifically designed to replace craft autonomy and exclusive control by managerial control of hiring, training and promotion to higher grades of skill and workshop organisation'.[1] This article, in common with a number of other authors' works,[2] examines Hobsbawm's notion of specifically designed labour policies in the light of more detailed evidence. An overview is provided of the industrial relations in British railway workshops from their beginnings until 1914. While the central theme of the article is the formation of labour policies by management, some additional observations are made concerning the difficulties of analysing labour relations at grass-roots level, and the functioning of 'factory politics'.

The comparative neglect of labour relations in railway workshops is hardly surprising in view of the approach taken to the history of labour relations in Britain before the mid-1970s. Most writers prior to that time were concerned with institutional histories of trade unions, employers' associations and government.[3] As a result their works reveal very little about life on the shop-floor. Some studies, of course, do dwell on labour relations, but often matters are represented in a static manner, as unadaptive to changing conditions. Railway workshop employees likewise, despite their high level of trade union membership, are seen as largely unchanging in their outlook. Acquiescent in labour matters (there were only three or four sectional strikes within the workshops throughout the years 1838–1914) workshopmen were also seen as being deferential in religion and politics. More recent studies of workers and the workplace in other industries are far more fruitful in pointing to the potential complexities both of railway company labour policies and 'worker responses'. Patrick Joyce for example, has demonstrated the importance of the 'milieux of work' in nineteenth century 'factory politics'.[4] However, as will be seen below, the connections between work and employee deference were, in the case of the railway workshops at least, deeper than and different from those proposed in Joyce's model. The current debates concerning labour markets and the labour process have also generated ideas which are of particular value to the study of railway workshop labour relations and factory life.

This study adds to the body of recent work which has brought a richer understanding of labour markets, the labour process and worker responses to managerial encroachment. The structure of the locomotive engineering industry is outlined in section I. Labour recruitment, the labour market and workshop organisation are considered in section II. Use is made of some of the ideas developed by Melling and Fitzgerald concerning managerial strategies aimed at gaining control of the labour market.[5] In section III, the discussion centres on management and the labour process, continuing the line of enquiry begun by Hobsbawm and Braverman and subsequently taken up and contested so vigorously by scholars such as Gospel, Littler, Harrison and Zeitlin.[6] Worker responses to managerial strategies are considered in section IV, including union, political and community issues. The various strands of the article are drawn together in section V and their importance discussed in the light of subsequent events.

I. Locomotive Engineering in Britain

The establishment of the workshops of Britain's railway companies was, with a few exceptions, a product of the 'Railway Boom' of the late 1830s and 1840s, and especially of the peak expansion years of 1839–1842. During this period, investment in railways grew from virtually nothing in 1834, to an average of £32 million a year by 1849. The length of both the entire railway system and many individual companies lines also increased considerably.[7]

Britain's private locomotive-building sector had been established during the 1820s and 1830s, developing out of the general engineering industry as the first period of increased demand for locomotives created the need for specialisation.[8] Early firms included the famous Robert Stephenson Company established in 1823, Sharp, Roberts and Co. (1830) and Charles Tayleur's 'Vulcan Foundry' (1830) as well as numerous small firms which were probably little more than 'jobbing foundries'. The exact number of private companies which existed during the railways' earliest years is uncertain, but the Great Western Railway (GWR) bought locomotives from 12 different firms in 1851. By 1900 there were probably more than 250 private firms in Britain.[9]

Such firms may have been numerous, some such as Stephenson's, having quite a large output, but with the next surge of locomotive demand in the years 1839–42 no private firm could fully meet the individual needs of one of the new larger railway companies, especially while they were fulfilling existing contracts with other companies.[10] This obliged companies to place orders with a number of separate firms, a factor which further complicated the companies' contractual difficulties. Competition for private firms supply presumably also raised prices and stalled delivery dates.[11] Integration of locomotive-building into the railway companies' existing activities of locomotive and rolling stock maintenance, the next stage of development for the locomotive-building industry, not only eradicated many of these problems, but gave the companies various advantages in the costing and supplying of loco-motives.

The railway companies' decision to build their own steam-engines and rolling-stock therefore created a locomotive manufacturing indus-try which was, with its private and company sectors, distinctive to Great Britain. Private companies continued to be centred in the long-established engineering areas of the North-East, Yorkshire and Lan-cashire, serving the overseas' and specialist market, and on occasions, home railway companies.[12] In contrast, railway company establishments were more widely dispersed. Being strategically located on their compa-nies' lines, they acted as both manufacturing and maintenance centres for their companies. Their product markets were also distinctive. Serving, at least after 1876, the demands of their parent company alone, the workshops were almost . . . 'an industry within an industry'.[13]

Constant and predictable demand also ensured that the railway com-panies' workshops were both larger and more technically advanced than many of their private counterparts. Initial investment was large, Swindon Works costing £35,290 to build and equip in 1843 and Crewe £109,482. Each contained some of the most advanced machine-tools then produced.[14] Workforces were also larger than those of private companies, as well as being highly variegated occupationally, a result of the shops' multi-staged manufacturing and repair processes.[15] So variously skilled, the 'shopmen' were represented by some 30 different craft and general trade unions by 1914. Thus by 1919, the railway com-pany workshops employed 135,000 men in 800 different workshops or depots, owned by a plethora of railway companies.[16]

II. Labour Recruitment and Workshop Organisation

One of the greatest problems facing Britain's early railway companies was that of gaining and disciplining a labour force. Initial railway recruitment took place when industrial discipline was relatively new and, more importantly for the works, when skilled engineering workers were in short supply.[17] Railway workers were drawn from two sources. Line and traffic workers came from the ranks of the unskilled, the railway companies training them themselves. The early railway company work-shops' labour needs were very different. There unionised craftsmen, trained elsewhere in the engineering industry and therefore members of an external labour market, were sought.

With their disparate labour demands, specific managerial design should have produced very different labour strategies in the workshops and on the line. Contemporary engineering employers, as Melling notes, attempted to gain control of their labour supply by creating or dominating local skilled labour markets through the granting of various welfare provi-sions. Railways however retained the services of their general workers through pay and promotion incentives, thus establishing an 'internal labour market' within each railway company.[18] In fact, while the railways adopted both these very specific strategies, line recruitment policies were often inappropriately extended into the companies' shops.

Britain's early railway companies had few precursors on which to model their labour recruitment policies. Only the Army and the East India Company had had similar experience of employing and disciplining such a large workforce. Indeed, both these organisations provided many of the railway companies' early managerial personnel.[19] Another managerial paradigm constantly presented to the railways by contemporaries, concerned by the social dislocation they saw the railway engendering, was that of an idealised paternalistic society of eighteenth-century rural England.[20]

Army-like discipline and paternalism therefore became the basis of all railway companies' industrial relations from their beginnings until the introduction of a new system of relations early in the present century. The vision of discipline and natural hierarchy which both of these models provided was most useful to early railway companies. To the lowly placed within the company, the railways' promise of promotion for obedience and loyalty in menial tasks aided public safety on the permanent-way. George Findlay, the General Manager of the L & NWR from 1881–92 used this army metaphor in his manual on railway management, instructing his officers to: 'Let servants know that there is a field marshal's baton in every private's knapsack'. Company paternalism was also seen to bring other results, the officers' '. . . constant study to maintain cordial and friendly relations with the individual worker . . .' militating against collective worker action.[21]

Company patronage governed a key mechanism in generating an internal labour market, the railways' appointments and promotions system. Work in the early companies was only granted after would-be employees had petitioned company directors, or in the case of the workshops, applied to company officers. Promotion was also only made on official recommendation. Patronage was also a vital component of the companies' appeals and discipline system. If an individual worker had a complaint he could make an appeal to the company directors via his immediate superior. Collective appeals were made by a deputation of men presenting a memorial of complaint. Such memorials were only permitted after a mass petition, or in the case of the London and North-Western Railway Co. (L & NWR) after 1880, when an industrial ballot had determined that the complaint was a concern of a majority of workers.[22] These labour policies, so well adapted to the needs of wider railway enterprise, were extended to all company workshops, despite their inappropriateness to their employment conditions, internal promotion being extremely limited there. Company records show that men of the North-Eastern Railway Co.'s shops at Darlington, Gateshead, Shildon and West Hartlepool petitioned their directors on a number of occasions, as did those of the Great Northern's shop at Darlington, the Great Western's Swindon works, and the L & NWR's Wolverton and Crewe shops.[23] Most usually, petitions were received from men of similar trades, as in the case of the wagon and machine-shop fitters at Gateshead in 1871. The subject of the workshops' memorials varied from demands for wage rises and reduction of working hours, as in the workshops' Nine Hour Campaigns of 1871, to a call for improved workplace safety, which the men of the Great Western Co.'s Swindon workshops made in 1848 and again during 1867.[24]

The railway companies were far more selective in the implementation of their second recruitment strategy. 'Welfarism', the companies' 'ex gratia' provision of benefits such as insurance societies, sick funds and above all pensions, had similar aims to the railways' appointment and appeals system. As early as 1848, the L & NWR had recognised that such societies presented yet another means of establishing and maintaining an internal labour market. By the late 1880s, welfarism was being used to combat New Unionism.[25] Prolific in their provision to all other railway departments, the companies' workshop men received few of these benefits. The majority of the workshop pension funds were not established until after regrouping. As late as 1923, the GWR recorded that '. . . shop staff are our only employees who cannot qualify for pension benefit . . .'[26] The only exception to this rule was the case of the L & NWR, which established a contributory pension fund for its shopmen in 1883.

Another welfare benefit which was extended to the workshops was that of insurance. The Great Eastern (GER), L & NWR and London, Brighton and South Coast (LBSCR) companies set up workshop insurance after the Railway Companies' Association's long campaign had permitted railways to 'contract-out' of the Employers' Liability Act of 1880.[27]

The reason for the shopmen's exclusion from welfare benefits appeared obvious to contemporaries. George Findlay, together with a later witness to the Industrial Court of 1919, complained that shopmen too often moved on to work elsewhere to make a welfare scheme viable within the works. In contradiction to these claims, trade union and company records alike testified to the shopmen's long-service.[28] Most probably, the question of the length of service will not be answered until some current research is completed, but there were other reasons for the workshops' exclusion from welfare benefits.[29] By the time of such schemes' introduction, the railway companies had developed far more efficient strategies for recruiting workshop labour, namely the use of company 'welfare provisions', especially as seen in the companies' establishment of their 'railway towns'.

With their decisions to newly establish or relocate their workshops at strategic points of their networks British railway companies created a new urban phenomenon, the 'railway town'. In settlements such as Wolverton (established 1838), Crewe (1843), Swindon (1842), and later Horwich (1884) and Eastleigh (1897) initial housing, churches, schools, hospitals and 'civic buildings' in the form of Mechanics' or

Literary Institutes were all paternalistic gifts of the company (see Appendix; Table 1). Even water and gas were supplied as by-products of the workshops' own demands for such utilities. Local and works-based organisations were also supported by the companies' 'ex gratia' grants. The need for company benevolence in these communities was obvious, for as Hudson observes of Swindon, '. . . without the railway village, the workshops could hardly have operated'.[30] No railway company recorded its aims in establishing a railway colony, but no doubt the results of such large investments were carefully calculated. The strategy soon proved successful. In removing their workshops to such isolated sites, the companies had created reservoirs of skilled labour within their new worker communities. The new workforces were loyal and obedient, one of the first railway colonies, established in 1838, reporting, 'We are beginning to find the economic benefits to the establishment at Wolverton . . . there is not a single person who would not willingly and gladly perform extra service when called upon'.[31]

By the 1880s, the railway companies had even more clearly created a captive pool of labour in their company towns. Trade unionists of both Crewe and Derby reported that their members were reluctant to take any industrial action because 'they had been in the works all their lives and knew no other'.[32] Unlike their predecessors, who had acquired their skills in long-established engineering areas such as Lancashire and the North-East, the shopmen, as the 1881 Census Enumerator reports for Crewe and Swindon both demonstrate, were predominantly trained by the railway companies themselves. With this restriction of the skilled workers' mobility and the control of apprenticeship the railway companies had robbed the skilled works' men of the nineteenth-century craft unions' leading strategy of controlling their trade's labour supply.[33] Company dominance was established not just for one generation, but with the control of apprenticeship, for many generations to come. The strategy of establishing railway colonies was also more appreciated by this time, John Ramsbottom consulting F.W. Webb, Crewe's Chief Mechanical Engineer (CME), on how the establishment of a new railway town at Horwich might best advantage the Lancashire and Yorkshire Company.[34] Another result of this strategy was the pattern of railway town politics. Continued political dominance gave the companies power to prevent alternative centres of employment from being established in their communities while also limiting local rate levels, an important consideration for the 'heavy ratepaying' companies. This dominance was, as will be seen in part IV, more of a product of workers' economic and political powerlessness than of their deference, as Joyce would maintain. Thus at Swindon, company employees ensured that the 'railway interest' and therefore their livelihood, was maintained by making their Chief Mechanical Engineer, Daniel Gooch, their member of parliament from 1865 to 1880.[35] In other famous railway centres, 'company interest' dominated municipal politics. Tory railway officials, George Hudson, the 'Railway King', and after 1848, George Leeman, 'ruled' York for some 50 years, while CME Webb was dubbed 'the Uncrowned King of Crewe' because of his indirect dominance of the town through the 'Independent Railway Company Party'.[36]

The workshop organisation of this newly recruited workforce was another problem for railway companies. In the works, shop-floor labour supervision was not carried out by company officers but by the piece-masters or foremen, supervisory personnel with delegated managerial authority. In 'piecemastering' or subcontracting, a skilled worker sub-employed a team of workers, training, supervising and paying them. Being paid on the basis of output or piecework, the subcontractor also took on the work of costing a job and obtaining raw materials, any miscalculations being passed on to the piecemaster through loss of profit. Foremen, as direct employees of the companies, did not subemploy workers, but were responsible for hiring, training and disciplining their workshop's men. The allocation of work, piecework prices and time-work along with the supply of materials and flow of work was also part of their duties.

The form of supervision selected to manage a workshop during the works' earlier years appears to have been dependent on a number of factors concerning the particular crafts' local labour market, production process risks and the level and constancy of product demand. At Swindon for example, the 'Fawcett List', reveals that in the early works, piecemastering was confined to six out of the 14 shops. These shops' production processes of wheel-making, forging, founding and boilermaking carried a high degree of risk in their execution. The use of subcontracting therefore passed the cost of any failure on to the piecemaster. Piecemastering was also an important recruitment strategy, highly skilled workers only being attracted to the new and isolated works by piecemastering's profit incentive. As these production processes became less risky and their workforces more stable, piecemastering at Swindon ceased. By 1865, the rule of the foreman had apparently totally replaced subcontracting.[37]

Subcontracting was also the most prevalent form of workshop employment at Derby and Wolverton but for very different reasons than at Swindon. At Derby, piecemastering was present from the works establishment, contracts between the company and gangs of locomotive erectors and wheel-turners being traceable as early as 1850. Here subcontracting did not end in the 1860s, but continued until the introduction of a more systematic piecework system during the 1890s. Only in the boilermaking and paint shops was subcontracting piecework abandoned in favour of time work, a step taken in the 1850s in an attempt to restore quality levels. The reason for the longevity of piecemastering at Derby lay in local labour market conditions. Piecemasters were encouraged to subemploy members of their own families, an ideal means of recruiting skilled men in the face of competition from other engineering firms in the city.[38]

At the L & NW Railway's works at Wolverton, purely a wagon and carriage works after the removal of all the company's locomotive-building and repair work to Crewe in 1867, subcontracting probably provided the company with a means to meet fluctating demands, contracted workers being more easily laid off. As at Derby, Wolverton's subcontractors were also important labour recruiters, apprenticeships being granted by the piecemaster and not the company as late as 1899. Wolverton's piecemasters also had another hold on their workers, for they paid them in tokens which were only redeemable at the master's own village shops.[39]

In all other railway works the foreman was the leading workshop supervisor. At Crewe, for example, subcontractors were only employed in a few sections of the works, notably the rail rolling mill and the Bessemer steel plant where production risks were high. Established at the same time as Swindon, and equally as isolated, Crewe never needed subcontracting as a recruitment strategy, many of the works' original employees being transferred from the Grand Junction Railway company's existing shops at Edgehill. The foreman was also the leading shopfloor authority in the North-Eastern Railway Co.'s (NER) works at York, Gateshead and Darlington, traditional engineering areas where skilled labour was plentiful.

By the 1890s the foreman had become the most important shopfloor authority in all company workshops, with subcontracting only being carried out in the workshops' more peripheral production processes such as brickmaking and wagon construction. However, increased company bureaucracy and the introduction of new grades of workshop-based managers, employed to implement new piecework systems, were beginning seriously to restrict the foreman's jurisdiction in 'his own shop'.

III. Management and the Labour Process

A final problem for company workshop management was that of gaining closer control of the labour process. In all other areas of railway enterprise, the pattern of work had been established by the companies themselves. However in the companies' workshops the pace of work, its method of execution, the whole 'inner life of the workshop', were determined by the skilled workers' craft autonomy and tradition. If the railway companies were ever to control work and costs, craft autonomy had to be at least partially replaced by managerial control.

For the railway companies, there were three strategies by which this could be achieved. Increased workshop supervision, in the form of the piecemaster or foreman's direct supervision, or indirectly through the implementation of piecework, did much to increase managerial control. Workshop rules also presented a means of increasing indirect control by the transfer of craft pride and loyalty to the company. Finally, the labour process itself could be further divided by some bureaucratic, supervisory or technical means.[40]

It was the first of these methods which was most extensively employed. The implementation or increase of piecework gave management opportunities to further divide and circumscribe the labour process, while 'payment by results' regulated work pace. Jefferys, drawing on the evidence of the Amalgamated Society of Engineers' (hereafter ASE) 'Return on Trade Customs' concludes that 'some of the larger locomotive building centres returned a higher than national average proportion of workers on piece work . . .'[41] Swindon had the highest level of piecework, with 50 per cent of its ASE members being employed by such a method, followed by the LB & SCR's Brighton works (20 per cent), and then Crewe, Wolverton and Doncaster (11 per cent each). With such levels a majority of the workshops' Society men obviously were employed on a 'time-rate' and so were free from the companies' attempts to more closely control their work.

Details of other workshops' payment systems are more fragmentary. At York, time-work was the rule for highly skilled men, and individual piecework for all other of workers, the ASE's strike of 1881 being an attempt to prevent piecework from being extended to the society's members. The situation at the company's Darlington works is even more uncertain. Despite Jefferys' claim that piecework of any kind was rare in 1861, a notebook kept at the Public Records Office suggests that individual piecework for most trades was well established by the late 1860s.[42] This notebook was the property of a 'chargeman', presumably a skilled worker, who, under the command of the shop foreman, was responsible for allocating work and piecework prices to the shopmen.

The late 1880s and 1890s saw the introduction of new payment systems which further intensified the indirect supervision of the labour process. Part of a general trend in the British engineering industry, these systems, together with new scientific work methods and technology, were adopted to combat the effects of economic depression and foreign competition. Elsewhere in the engineering industry, this drive to increase managerial prerogatives was to culminate in the ASE lockout of 1897–98, an action in which neither the railway companies' works nor their employees engaged.

The railway companies' workshops did adopt some of these new payment methods but somewhat contradictory evidence suggests that the most famous of these, the premium bonus system, was only employed for a short time there. Some form of systematic piecework was certainly introduced into Crewe and Derby works by 1895, the Webbs' respondents of both ASE branches recording that 'work in the workshops is piecework on a bonus system'.[43] However in the case of Derby there is some doubt that this was of the premium bonus type, two later documents suggesting that the system was actually introduced by Works Manager George Deeley between 1903 and 1907.[44]

By 1911, individual piecework appears to have become far more prevalent than the premium bonus system in most workshops, the further division of the labour process making this form of piecework easier to implement. A Darlington works' notebook of that date details the methods used to pay the many different shopmen, not only in the North-Eastern works themselves but in many other railway company and engineering workshops.[45] This records that premium bonus was only paid in 78 out of 238 cases. Only at the Midland's Derby works, where premium bonus was paid in eight out of 15 cases, and at Armstrong-Whitworths' Newcastle factory (12 out of 14 cases) was the premium bonus used to any degree. At Darlington itself, premium bonuses were probably never paid. Highly systematised individual piecework books, giving prices for every task involved in the manufacture of each of the company's class of locomotives, were clearly used in the works throughout the 1890s and 1900s. Further statistics from the NER show the use of individual piecework rising during the 1900s, the levels worked by all grades of workers employed at Darlington being increased from 67 per cent in 1906 to 85 per cent by 1912.[46]

As a means of reducing craft autonomy and solidarity in the workplace company workshop rules were in part highly successful. The rules which most aided management were those which attempted to undermine craft pride and solidarity, replacing it with pride and identification with the railway company. In the first instance, the 'inner life of the workshop' the traditional basis of craft action was undermined by those rules which insisted that all meal and tea breaks should be taken in the works' canteen and not in the shops or work areas. At Derby even the men's family unity was threatened by the company's employment of family heads as subemploying piecemasters. Craft unity was weakened further by individual workshops' occupational structures, many of the works' manufacturing processes obliging men of different trades to work together. Certain shop workers therefore began to identify more strongly with their company than their craft. In company sponsored competitions, such as brass band displays or football matches, workers represented their workshop or works and not their trade or craft. The shopmen's craft solidarity severely weakened, craft pride was often converted to company pride through the prestige of the steam-locomotive, so clearly a product of a 'company' of men of different trades and talents and not of a single craft. Hobsbawm also claims that craft pride was turned to company property by the use of workshop rules which obliged skilled workers to provide their own tools.[47] In fact, the question of tool ownership and the transfer of craft pride was far more complex than this. Company obligation merely enforced craft tradition, while such an order in no ways removed any of the worker's discretion in tool selection and use. Craft pride and independence were far more likely to be undermined by the increased use of shop tools or, as in the case of a rule at Swindon, the restriction on the making of tools. Tools made during apprenticeship traditionally set a man up in his craft for life. However, both these rules and other shop rules concerning the quality of workmanship were more likely to be counter-productive to company

control, representing an obvious attack on craft autonomy and an insult
to the skilled workers' values.

The final managerial strategy for gaining further control of the labour
process was to divide further the labour process. During the workshops' earlier days, bureaucracy was usually used to achieve this. The
implementation or increased use of individual piecework, for instance,
permitted companies not only to further divide, but also to more closely
plan and direct work. This occurred in Crewe works as early as 1848.
Skilled fitters, known as 'vicemen' and employed on piecework were set
to repeatedly turning out a single item such as a regulator or a whistle.[48]
Bureaucratic division of labour by the use of individual piecework
undoubtedly reached its greatest extent with the NE company's comprehensive system in Darlington during the 1890s. Occasionally in the
years before the 1890s the workshop management found opportunity
to transfer sections of the further divided work process to lesser skilled
workers. At Doncaster works, the Great Northern company gave some
of the blacksmiths' work to their semi-skilled assistants during a blacksmiths' strike in 1870, while a similar action at York in 1881 temporarily
replaced fitters with semi-skilled assistants, but with some unfortunate
results.[49]

Bureaucratic division of work and the transfer of tasks to other
workers came into its own in the railway workshops during the 1890s,
when new systematic piecework was accompanied by the introduction
of task or team work. Here individual workers or teams were repeatedly
kept to performing a single task or section of a manufacturing process.[50]
With the general skill level reduced, semi-skilled workers such as fitters'
assistants, or in foundry and forges, boys, were brought into the workshops in ever increasing numbers. By 1904, nearly 14 per cent of all
railway workshop employees were boys.[51]

The introduction of new technologies presented limited opportunities
for management to gain further control of the labour process. In boilermaking for example it was increased workshop organisation and not new
technology that further divided the labour process, the introduction of
hydraulic riveters in the late 1860s and pneumatic machines in 1900
simply speeding the rate of boiler construction. However, the super-
seding of old traditional ironmaking methods by various steelmaking
processes during the 1860s did do much to replace craft autonomy with
managerial control, but this production process was only carried out in
larger company workshops such as Crewe and Swindon. Technology
also did little to further divide the labour process in company workshops' finishing and fitting trades. At Crewe, Derby and Swindon,[52]
all machine-tools introduced before the late 1870s merely turned fitters' and turners' hand work to machine work. Jigs and templates
were introduced into Derby and Crewe works from the mid-1860s
onwards when the standardisation of locomotive components began.
This trend increased throughout the period under review, but their use,
while lessening skill levels, failed to transfer work to workers who were

more amenable to workshop management.[53] The first effective transfer of skilled work to semi-skilled workers occurred when the introduction of milling machines in the late 1870s and early 1880s took away the turner's fine-finishing work.[54] In other sectors of the British engineering industry it was the introduction of automatic turret and capstan lathes in the late 1890s which is usually considered to have most undermined craftsmens' skill and discretion. Despite standardisation, the railway companies' relatively limited product market meant that adaptability of men and machines was preferable to the new automatic machine-tools' specificity. Therefore in the railway works apparently few of these machine-tools were introduced until the 1910s, while the planning of such work by the companies' own 'progress offices' in the form of 'speed and feed tables' was probably not used until a similar date.[55] At the railway company workshops therefore discretion in using machine-tools continued to be very much the property of skilled workers well into the present century.[56]

IV. Politics, Community, and Rank and Fileism

The companies were not, however, the only authors of industrial relations within the company workshops during the period 1839–1914. The men of the workshops were not after all, 'so many pieces of human machinery', to be used by the companies.[57] Despite their powerlessness, the men of the workshops developed their own strategies. Failing to challenge company power head on, these strategies, often stemming from the legacy of trade unionism or nonconformity which workers brought with them to these new works, sustained an independent culture within the worker communities.[58] In time, this working-class independence was to spell the end of railway companies' dominance of such communities, both within the workplace and in local politics.

The key to company power in the railway workshops lay not in the works themselves but in these worker communities and the degree of dominance companies had over the local labour market. There were of course a number of traditional strategies by which craft unions attempted to retain control of their own particular trade's labour market but these appear to have fallen quickly into disuse in the companies' workshops. In the workshops' early days men can be traced 'tramping' to other places of employment through the monthly reports of the men's trade union, the Steam-Engine Makers' Society (SEM). By the 1880s, tramping had ceased but the SEM still published monthly bulletins on where work was available.[59] However, while direct evidence is still to be gathered, there is much to suggest that by this time, relatively few works' men ever moved on from the railway shops. Works' craft unions also failed to press for the regulation of apprenticeship numbers, an action which would have resulted in much unemployment amongst the young men of the communities. A final possible strategy was that of setting up alternative places of work for the communities' men. Although much

supported by political groups which opposed the companies' dominance
in such towns, nothing ever came of such plans.

Independent working-class culture was far more successful in undermining the companies' dominance in other areas of life outside the
works. With their history of working-class independence, newcomers
to these communities often responded to the companies' benevolent
paternalism by establishing their own institutions. Working-class collective action provided a wealth of amenities in all the railway centres,
from chapels and clubs, to cooperatives and trade unions. Craft trade
unions, unlike the railway companies themselves, established superannuation and pension funds for their members, while local building
societies provided an alternative to company housing. In Swindon, for
instance, 60 per cent of housing stock was owner-occupied by 1900.[60] The
alternative social life and culture of these institutions formed a basis for
political opposition to company dominance in the railway towns.[61]

This working-class independence was to have important implications
for the functioning of 'factory politics', at least in the 'railway towns'.
Railway company paternalism failed to create the 'total environment'
from which Joyce argues worker deference and therefore nineteenth-
century factory politics developed. 'Railway town politics' were not born
of deference, but rather of the workers' appreciation of the political
and economic realities of life in such towns. Often, especially during
the towns' early years, the 'Railway Interest' was the only form of
political representation open to shopmen. Even after local government
had become more representative and the men had been enfranchised,
political support of the railways continued through company influence
or coercion. Railway companies constantly reminded their workers
that failure to vote for the companies' political appointees would result
in economic difficulties for the company and therefore for its employees.
At best, they promised a rise in commodity prices through the increase
of railway freight rates. CME Webb warned that he 'would not be
responsible for what the directors might do in regard to putting on
the rates' if the workmen did not elected company officers during
Crewe's first town council elections in 1877.[62] At worst, they spoke
of the total removal of a workshop or depot, as in the case of the L
& NWR's Carlisle running shed in 1869.[63] This 'influencing' was also a
daily feature of life in the workshops, foremen and piecemasters using
their allocation of work, piecework prices and apprenticeships to gain
political support. Those who resisted and retained their own beliefs were
gradually 'screwed out of their places', being put to harsh low-paid work
until they finally left the workshops.[64] Rather interestingly, the type of
managerial figure employed in the workshops significantly altered the
pattern of a local community's politics. Foremen as direct employees of
the company used their influence as the company directed. The foremen
at Crewe were notorious not only for pressing their workers to vote for
the 'Independent Railway Company Party', but also for influencing them
in matters of religion, persuading them to attend the company-provided

church where CME Webb's brother was incumbent.[65] The more independent piecemasters at both Wolverton and Derby influenced workers for their own ends. Here they granted work to those men who were of the same denominational or political persuasion as they, or, as in the case of Wolverton's parliamentary election in the 1870s, trying to get the Liberal works' manager elected so that he could reward them with additional contracts of work. This influencing was only gradually ended by opposing political forces questioning or publicly denouncing the companies' domination.[66]

Inside the workshops themselves working-class culture, particularly in the form of craft unionism, did continue, but was often much subordinated to the company. Workplace worker strategies were often only successful when they spilled over into mass political action in the wider community. Attempts to counter managerial control of the labour process were particularly piecemeal and ineffective. Workshop authority in the person of the foreman or the piecemaster was commonly hated by workmen, but any defiance of them merely resulted in the workers' instant dismissal. Opposition to piecework was also difficult. Refusal to work for low piecework prices once again brought instant dismissal, as did any collusion between men to slow down the pace of work, a strategy used in all the workshops to obstruct the introduction of systematic piecework.[67] Occasionally workshopmen did take mass action against piecework. At York in 1881, members of the ASE struck work to try and prevent its introduction, while the 1889 piecework dispute at Crewe was only one of the campaigns which made up the town's 'Second Intimidation Affair'.[68] Of these actions, only that at York was successful.

While there were few if any means by which workers could defy the companies' workshop rules, under certain work conditions craft solidarity and autonomy could be preserved. This was especially true of the shops where the labour process dictated that men of the same trade worked together employed on a time-work basis. Such shops became important centres of independent working-class action, as in the case of the 'Blue Ribbon Gang' of one of Crewe's erecting shops. A group highly-skilled fitter-erectors well known for their support of Liberalism and nonconformity, their forcible dismissal from the works sparked off the town's 'Second Intimidation Affair'.[69] This workshop solidarity was short-lived, being undermined by the introduction of task and team work in the 1890s.

Despite the companies' actions craft unionism also continued in most shops, encouraged by the companies' dependence on workers' skill. Company rules of obligation of ownership and in the use of shop tools failed to remove the skilled worker's discretion in selecting and handling tools while the employment of machine-tools and task work merely restricted the breadth of the craftman's skill.

It was from the workshop craft unionism that the most long-standing and effective of the shopmen's works'-based strategies emerged. In a short time this strategy was to prove to be effective in determining the future of the railway communities' politics too. From the workshops' establishment the rank and file within craft unionism attempted to use the company-established industrial relations system to gain their own collective demands and trade union recognition. The earliest example of this occurred in Swindon in 1843, shopmen making a collective appeal for improved piecework prices. In 1853, men of the NER's York and Gateshead works made similar appeals, their Locomotive Superintendent Fletcher being instructed by the company's directors, 'not to take any united application or to meet any men as a body . . .'[70] as a measure against trade unionism.

The most dramatic demonstration of how workshop rank and fileism could effect politics and community took place during the 'Nine Hours Movement' of 1871. Practically every company shop took part in this, the shopmen petitioning their directors for a shorter working week by holding mass public meetings. At the Ashford, Earlestown, Stoke-on-Trent, Swindon and Wolverton workshops meetings were less obviously a product of trade union rank and fileism and local political action, although at York, Darlington and Swindon, the Movement was accompanied by demands for wage advances from the workshops' fitters and turners, a common feature of ASE action at this time. However, the largest meetings, held at Crewe and Derby, were led by worksmen who were radical in both their trade unionism and their politics. At Crewe, for example, 5,000 men met on the town square to be addressed by their local ASE branch officials, religious and political radicals and future founders of Crewe's Liberal party in 1872.[71] Derby's 'Nine Hour Movement' march to the works' manager's home was organised by the recently formed Amalgamated Society of Railway Servants (ASRS); the union, actually formed in Derby the preceding year, influencing politics in the city from then on.

Successful in attaining its immediate goal, a similar demonstration of rank and file trade unionism was not to be seen in the workshops until 1881. In that year, a body dubbing itself 'The Nine Hours Movement of the ASRS' called on shopmen to press for employer recognition of trade unions. The Movement was soon stopped, systematic victimisation of its members beginning after Fletcher, Superintendent of the NE company, had intercepted one of the Movement's broadsheets.[72]

Rank and fileism was revived in the 1880s–1890s. Its recovery was prompted by the establishment of company welfare schemes and the debate concerning employers' liability. As already noted, in the years prior to regrouping, only the L & NWR extended its pension fund to include its shopmen. It was compulsory and relatively costly to the men, who complained that few of them lived long enough to enjoy its benefits, and Crewe's ASE branches resolved both to end the pension fund and oppose the company politically.[73] Thus, Crewe's 'Pension Fund Dispute' of 1889, conducted simultaneously with campaigns against short-time working and the increase in piecework, sparked off the town's 'Second

Intimidation Affair' and a further attempt to prove that the company's political dominance was a product of workplace coercion and not natural deference.[74]

The Pension Fund was finally dissolved after a balloting of its members, including the employees of other company workshops, determined its unpopularity. None of the works' men's other demands were met, and the company's political hold was not broken until 1890. There were other important by-products of the dispute however; the rise of New Unionism and the formation of a permanent deputation of men within the works.[75]

In all other workshops and companies, trade union rank and fileism was much encouraged by the ASRS's campaign against the Employers' Liability Bill of 1880. Employees of the L & NWR, one of the three railway companies to 'contract out' of the bill, also fought a fierce battle to prove that the company ballot, held to test employees' opinion of 'contracting out' of the Liability Act, had been rigged. Worker opposition was reported throughout the line, and mass meetings of 2,000 and 1,000 men respectively were held at Liverpool and Crewe. The men memoralised the company's directors, but to no avail, their letters of appeal were not even read by the company.[76]

Pressure for workshop union recognition and the establishment of some form of collective bargaining gained even more momentum during the 1900s. In 1901 craft trade unionists in the L & NWR's shops attempted to use the company's appeal system to gain union recognition. The superintendent of the company's Earlestown Works complained that a group of Wolverton men had visited his and all other shops to 'get up a petition' to this end. This wider attempt to gain recognition within the L & NWR failed, but union recognition was granted to all workshop unions, craft and general alike, in Crewe in 1911. This 'Joint Committee of all workshop unions' was formed after the company's plans to dismiss over 500 men from its overstaffed works had caused a public outcry in the town. Similar 'Joint Committees' were established in other companies' workshops a little later.[77] Pressure for trade union representation within the railway workshops also came form the workshops' unskilled workers and their unions. In 1907, the Railway Conciliation Scheme had given the ASRS negotiation rights for all its members except for those within the workshops, the only exception to this being the labourers of Horwich works who took a case to arbitration in August 1911.[78] With this the ASRS began to recruit semiskilled and unskilled workshopmen even more fiercely, demanding that a similar form of collective bargaining should be established in the works. By 1913, both the ASRS and the 'Craft Union Committee', the newly formed national federation of some 30 workshop craft unions, had begun to clamour for a new system of industrial relations within the workshops.[79] The 'Craft Union Committee' was just about to launch a programme of demands when the First World War broke out, and trade union activity was suspended for its duration.

V. Response and Resolution

Pre-planned and, in all but a few exceptions, ideally adapted to the companies' needs, British railway company workshops' first era of labour policies were very much of the companies' specific design. The workshops' product markets, each catering for the demands of its parent railway company, together with their dominance of local labour markets, also added to the companies' hegemony in labour matters. However, even in this first, company-dominated era, the companies were not the sole arbiters of workshop relations, workshop employees making small but calculated responses to management labour strategies. In time these 'worker strategies', especially their trade union rank and fileism and its appropriation of the company appeals mechanism, brought an end to this old paternalistic system of industrial relations and the employer politics which accompanied it.

By 1914 workshopmen were clamouring for the replacement of this system by a totally new one of collective bargaining and trade union recognition. Such a system was gained under the Industrial Court of 1919, but it was not fully implemented in every company shop until the late 1920s, a result of shopfloor resistance and inter-union rivalry.

Wartime conditions in the railway company workshops did not end pre-war worker demands but, as in other industries, encouraged them. With the need for a nationally coordinated rail network the control of the railways passed to the 'Railway Executive', a board of railway company general managers. Workshop industrial relations finally came under the control of the 'Committee of Production', a body set up by the Munitions Act, in 1915. Under the committee, shop committees were set up for the skilled men represented by the 'Craft Union Committee', now dubbed 'The Railway Shop Union Organisation Committee'.[80] No such privileges were extended to the works' unskilled men, members of the National Union of Railwaymen, a successor of the ASRS, which by then had 52,000 members.

With war's end and the decontrol of British railways, planning for the railways' and workshops' future took on a new urgency. However, the idea of nationalisation was soon abandoned, the railway companies being regrouped into four new private companies, the London, Midland and Scottish, Great Western, Southern and London and North-Eastern. These new companies were anxious to renegotiate workshop industrial relations, establishing collective bargaining as they were obliged to pay works' employees enhanced war bonuses until a new system was introduced. Hostility between the craft unions and the NUR, both at national level and locally, was to prevent the full implementation of this scheme until the late 1920s.

Inter-union rivalry for the right to represent workshopmen had begun before the war. The method of arbitration and wage standardisation to be adopted was also a point of contention, the craft unions advocating district rates and the NUR line rates and a conciliation system similar to that set up on the railways in 1907. Between 1915 and 1920, union relations had grown so bad that they refused to negotiate with one another, the railway companies complaining of union obstruction.

A system of collective bargaining was finally formulated in 1922 under the auspices of the Industrial Relations Court, but local inter-union rivalry and works' mens' mistrust of company policy further stalled its implementation. At Swindon, for example, a total of 370 erecting shopmen, skilled, semi-skilled and unskilled alike, held a 'stay in strike' after men had been expelled from the ASE for criticising the local branches' rejection of the new system.[81] Regrouping of the railway companies also brought workshop reorganisation. Crewe, Derby and Swindon works were each extended. Their work and repair processes were also rationalised into timed operations, new machine-tools introduced and the use of 'speed and feed charts' and progress chasing drastically increased. At other workshops, notably those of the LNER, reorganisation instituted far fewer technical changes, but still took place.[82] With such threatening changes to work patterns taking place in the workshops during an era when the general tenor of industrial relations was stormy, company workshops became militant. During 1926 some 80 per cent of once-acquiescent railway shopmen supported the General Strike. Eventually the new plan for industrial relations was fully accepted and introduced, thus establishing the company workshops' first nationally-based collective bargaining system. The shopmen's longstanding trade union rank and fileism had finally attained its goal.

Royal Holloway and Bedford New College, London

NOTES

1. E.J. Hobsbawm, 'Artisans and Labour Aristocrats', in E.J. Hobsbawm, *Worlds of Labour: Further Studies in the History of Labour* (1984), p.264.
2. See my thesis, D.K. Drummond, 'Crewe – The Society and Culture of a Railway Town, 1842–1914' (unpublished Ph.D. thesis, University of London, 1986), and the current work of Professor P. Bagwell on Doncaster Works, George Revill, Department of Geography, University of Loughborough, work for Ph.D. on Derby works. Many thanks to both Professor Bagwell and George Revill for their discussions, and to Drs Charles Harvey and John Turner, Department of History, Royal Holloway and Bedford New College, University of London, for their help and encouragement in suggesting this article and seeing it through to completion.
3. See John Turner, 'Review. Man and Braverman: British Industrial Relations', *History*, Vol.XXVIII, No.28 (June 1985), pp.236–42, for very useful discussion on recent historiography, and the interaction of the labour market, labour process and politics.
4. P. Joyce, *Work, Society and Politics: The Culture of the Factory in Late Victorian England* (1980), especially Chs.5 and 6.
5. See J. Melling, 'Employers Industrial Welfare and the Struggle for Workplace Control in British Industry, 1880–1920', in H. Gospel and C. Littler (eds.), *Managerial Strategies and Industrial Relations: An Historical and Comparative study* (1983) and R. Fitzgerald, *British Labour Management and Industrial Welfare, 1846–1939* (1987) and 'Employers' Labour Strategies, Industrial Welfare and the Response to New

Unionism at Bryant and May, 1880–1930', in C. Harvey and J. Turner (eds.), *Labour and Business in Modern Britain* (1989).

6. H. Braverman, *Labour and Monopoly Capitalism: The Degradation of Work in the Twentieth Century* (New York, 1974), E.J. Hobsbawm, 'Custom, Wages and Work Load' in E.J. Hobsbawm, *Labouring Men; Studies in the History of Labour* (1964), pp.344–71, C. Wrigley (ed.), *A History of British Industrial Relations, 1874–1914* (Brighton, 1982), H. Gospel and C. Littler (eds.), *Managerial Strategies and Industrial Relations* (1983), R. Harris and J. Zeitlin (eds.), *Divisions of Labour: Skilled Workers and Technological Change in Nineteenth-Century England* (Brighton, 1985).

7. T. Gourvish, *Railways and the British Economy, 1830–1914* (1980), p.12, Table 1.

8. See K. Burgess, 'Technical Change and the 1852 Lock out in the British Engineering Industry', *International Review of Social History*, Vol.XIV (1969), pp.215–36.

9. Public Record Office (hereafter PRO) RAIL 1008/83 – Great Western Railway Company report to the Board of Trade on the origins of their locomotives, 5 Dec. 1851, p.13 and p.237. James Lowe, *British Locomotive Builders* (Cambridge, 1975), pp.14–19 lists all private locomotive building companies which existed in Britain throughout the period. For details of the structure and location of the early private building sector see, B.J. Turton, 'The British Railway Engineering Industry: A Study in Economic Geography', *Tijdschrift Voor Economik and Sociale Geografie* (July–Aug., 1967), pp.193–206.

10. O. Williamson, *Markets and Hierarchies – Analysis and Anti-trust Implications: A Study in the Economics of Internal Organization* (New York, 1975), p.89.

11. Ibid, p.65.

12. Turton, loc. cit.

13. PRO RAIL 1025/98, *Decision of the Industrial Court No.728* (July 1922), p.71, evidence of Cramp of the NUR.

14. F.B. Head, *Stokers and Pokers, or the London and North-Western Railway, the Electric Telegraph, and the Railway Clearing House* (1849 edn., Reprint, Newton Abbot, 1968), p.110.

15. A.S. Peck, *The Great Western at Swindon* (Oxford, 1983), p.19 and for Crewe PRO RAIL 220/4 Grand Junction Railway Company Board Minutes, 10 May 1843. In 1900 Swindon works employed 14,000 workers. Neilson Reid and Company the largest private firm employed 3,500. See Peck, loc. cit., p.210 and J. Lowe. op. cit., p.8.

16. See PRO RAIL 1025/98 *Decision of Industrial Court No.728* (July 1922), Section II, pp.11–13, for details of trade unions, and PRO RAIL 1025/96, *Rates and conditions of railway shopmen* (Sept. 1921), p.71 for details of the number of men employed in various railway company establishments.

17. K. Burgess, *The Origins of British Industrial Relations: The Nineteenth-Century Experience* (1975), p.5.

18. Melling in Gospel and Littler (eds.), op. cit., p.64, Turner, *History* and Fitzgerald in Harvey and Turner, op. cit.

19. G. Turnbull, 'A Note on the supply of staff for the early railways', *Transport History* (Newton Abbot, 1968), pp.3–10.

20. PRO RAIL 1008/83 Transcript of Selected GWR Historical Letters, contains a letter written to the GWR by a 'Christian Lady' calling upon the company to look after its workers as a 'pastor would his flock'.

21. George Findlay, *The Working Management of an English Railway* (6th edition, 1889), pp.75 and 55.

22. P.W. Kingsford, *Victorian Railwaymen: The Emergence and Growth of Railway Labour, 1830–1879* (1970), Part 1 details how this system function in more general railway work.

23. Examples, Darlington Wagon Works, PRO RAIL 427/55 North-Eastern Railway Company Locomotive and Stores Committee, 14 June 1888, Minute No.273; York PRO RAIL 527/29 NE Railway Co. general minute book 12 Aug., 1870;

Gateshead PRO RAIL 527/30 NE Railway Co., 26 Jan. 1872, and RAIL 527/29 24 March 1871.

24. L.V. Grinsell, *A History of Swindon* (Swindon, 1950), p.103.

25. Fitzgerald in Harvey and Turner, op. cit.

26. PRO, RAIL 258/198 GWR company, file 'Pensions for Chargemen', 17 May 1940, p.2.

27. P.W.J. Bartrip and S.B. Burman, *The Wounded Soldiers of Industry: Industrial Compensation Policy, 1833–1897* (Oxford, 1983), Chaps.5 and 6, G. Alderman, *The Railway Interest* (Leicester, 1973), and for special details of the L & NWR's actions see, D.G. Hames, *The First British Workman's Compensation Act, 1897* (Yale University, 1968), pp.68–75.

28. British Library of Economic and Political Science (hereafter BLEPS) Webb MS Trade Union Collection E, Section A, Vol.XVI, p.207, Derby's ASE respondent said that workers had been 'brought up as lads here'. See also PRO, RAIL 1025/96 Appendix 29, 'statement showing long service of railway shops staff'.

29. My current project of computer-linking entries in the Crewe Works' Registers of employees 1870–1890 should answer many questions concerning such matters as recruitment and length of service in the railway workshops.

30. K. Hudson, 'The Early Years of the Railway Colony in Swindon', *Transport History*, Vol.1, No.2 (1968), p.132.

31. P.W. Kingsford, 'Labour Relations on the Railways, 1835–1875', *Journal of Transport History*, Vol.1 (1953), p.77.

32. BLEPS, Webb MS Trade Union Collection E, Section A, Vol.XVI, p.205, Crewe ASE respondent.

33. Analysis of Census enumerators' reports for both Swindon and Crewe show that the works' trained a large proportion of their own skilled workforce by the late 1870s. See Drummond, 'Thesis', Tables 2.16 and 2.17 for Crewe and Grinsell. op. cit., Tables, Appendix A. J. Hinton, *The First Shop Stewards' Movement* (1970), p.56 and G. Anderson, 'Some Aspects of the Labour Market in Britain *c.* 1870–1914', in Wrigley (ed.), op. cit., pp.1–19.,

34. H.A.V. Bulleid, *The Aspinall Era* (1967), p.80.

35. F.W.S. Craig, *British Parliamentary Election Results, 1832–1885* (1977).

36. For references to York, see A. Peacock, 'George Leeman and York Politics 1838–1880', in C.H. Feinstein (ed.), *York, 1831–1981: One Hundred Years of Scientific Endeavour and Social Change* (York, 1981), and for Crewe, Chaloner, op. cit., especially Chap.VI on the town's politics. *Crewe Chronicle*, 9 June 1906, dubbed Webb 'the Uncrowned King of Crewe' in his obituary. For further commentary on 'railway town politics' see H.J. Hanham, *Elections and Party Management: Politics in the time of Disraeli and Gladstone* (Sussex, 1978), Ch.4, Part IV.

37. PRO RAIL 264/254, Fawcett List of all Officers, Managers, Submanagers, Foremen and contractors, 1 Jan. 1843–31 Dec. 1865.

38. Information supplied by George Revill, and 'Strephon', 'Midland Railway Sketches', Reprinted from the *Sheffield Daily Telegraph* (1876).

39. K. Hudson, *Working to Rule. Railway Workshop Rules: A Study in Industrial Discipline* (Bath, 1970), p.49.

40. C. Littler, 'A Comparative Analysis of Managerial Structures and Strategies', in Gospel and Littler (eds.), op. cit., p.175.

41. M. and B. Jefferys, 'The Wages, Hours and Trade Customs of the Skilled Engineer in 1861', *Economic History Review*, 1st Series, Vol.XVII (1947), pp.27–44.

42. PPO, RAIL 527/1618 Piecework price book for Darlington works of the North-Eastern Railway Co., 1864.

43. BLEPS, Webb MS Trade Union Collection E, Section A, Vol.XVI, p.209.

44. See note 38, and PRO RAIL 527/1936 NE Railway Co. Darlington Works piecework book *c.* 1911 records that 'the premium bonus system was introduced into Derby a few years ago'.

45. Ibid.

28   LABOUR AND BUSINESS IN MODERN BRITAIN

46. PRO, RAIL 527/246 Chief Mechanical Engineer's half-yearly reports to the NE Railway Co., June 1907–12.
47. Hobsbawm, 'Artisans or Labour Aristocrats', p.264, and Hudson, loc. cit.
48. Head, op.cit., p.110.
49. PRO, RAIL 236/195 GNR Locomotive Committee Book No.2 for 1869–74, Minute No.269, 19 June 1870 for Doncaster and PRO, RAIL 527/1901, NER, Special file on the 'Nine Hour Movement' at York.
50. J.G. Sams, 'Recollection of Crewe, 1897–1902', *Railway Magazine*, Vol.LIV (1924) and Webb MS Trade Union Collection E, Section A, Vol.XVI, p.209, Crewe ASE respondent.
51. *Jackson Report* (PP, 1909, XLIV), p.124.
52. For Crewe see Drummond, thesis, pp.422–39 Addendum, List of Machine-Tools Introduced into Crewe works, 1843–1914; information for Derby from George Revill and to appear in his forthcoming thesis; for Swindon see PRO, RAIL 253/323 Tenders for Machinery, Swindon 1867–1916.
53. For details of the use of jigs and templates see J.Simmons, *The Railway in England and Wales 1830–1914*, Vol.I (Leicester, 1978), p.174; O.S. Nock, *Steam Locomotives: A Retrospect on the Works of the Great Railway Engineers* (1968), p.10 and J.A. Aspinall, Vice-President of the Mechanics' Institute, General Manager of the Lancashire and Yorkshire Railway, *Railway Magazine*, Vol.I (Dec. 1900), p.488.
54. Crewe works introduced a Profile Milling machine, which did this work in 1884. A similar machine was introduced into Swindon works in 1874. For details of the effects of the introduction of new machine-tools see A.L. Levine, 'Industrial Change and the effects on labour, 1900–1914' (unpublished Ph.D. Thesis, University of London, 1954).
55. PRO, RAIL 410/266, Locomotive Committee Minutes of L & NWR 1917, Min. No.29213, 15 1917.
56. See D.K. Drummond, 'Building a Locomotive: Skill and the Work Force in Crewe Locomotive Works, 1843–1914', *Journal of Transport History*, Vol.VII (March 1987), pp.1–29.
57. R.E. Pahl, *On Work: Historical, Comparative and Theoretical Approaches* (Oxford, 1988), p.170.
58. For evidence of the strength of nonconformity in many of these railway colonies, see Drummond, thesis, p.296, Table 6.2; F. Large, *Swindon Retrospect* (1970); and O.S. Richards, 'Methodism and the Railway: A Story of Wolverton', *Proceedings of the Wesley Historical Society*, Vol.XXXVII, Pt.I (Feb. 1969), pp.20–25. Evidence of the strength of trade union support in the early railway works is given in the 'Old Mechanics' union's vote on the motion to form the ASE, *A.S.E. Jubilee Souvenir*.
59. *S.E.M. Monthly Reports, 1888–1914* kept at the Bishopsgate Institute contains reports on the availability of work in the different locomotive-building centres, for example, *S.E.M. Quarterly Report*, October 1885 records that at Wolverton five SEM members had been paid off and that the works were on four days a week short time.
60. Grinsell, op. cit., p.71.
61. See Drummond, 'Thesis', Chs.6 and 7 and W.H. Chaloner, *The Social and Economic Development of Crewe, 1780–1923* (Manchester, 1950), Ch.VI.
62. Ibid., p.146, originally quoted in *Crewe Chronicle*, 4 July 1877 and Hanham, op. cit., p.90. Hanham suggests that 'putting on the rates' refered to men being dismissed from the Works and 'put on the parish' if they did not vote for company representatives. More likely, Webb was making reference to the railway's freight rates, which if raised, would increase the cost of practically all commodities and foodstuffs in Crewe.
63. Hanham, op. cit., Ch.4, Pt.IV.
64. See Chaloner, op. cit., Ch.VI and Drummond, thesis, Chs.6 and 7. During the height of the 'First Intimidation Affair in Crewe' the local Liberal newspaper used the headline, 'A Screw at Crewe', refering to company political coercion of its workers. (See *Crewe Chronicle*, 18 Oct. 1885.) Joyce also makes reference to this practice of 'Screwing workers out of their place', but apparently without seeing the full implications of this, Joyce, op. cit., p.217.

65. F. McKenna, *The Railway Workers* (1980), p.48.
66. Chaloner, op. cit., Ch.6.
67. J.B. Jefferys, *The Story of the Engineers* (1945), p.100.
68. PRO, RAIL 527/1901 NER, 'Nine Hours Movement' at York.
69. Drummond, 'Thesis', Chs.6 and 7.
70. PRO, RAIL 527/23 North-Eastern Railway Co. Locomotive and Stores Committee, 19 June 1853, Minute No.31.
71. See *The Beehive*, 11 Nov. 1871, p.4, for Manchester, Derby, Crewe, Ashford, Wolverton and Wolverhampton; *Beehive*, 18 Nov. 1871, p.4 for Stoke-on-Trent and Newton; 6 Jan. 1872, for Crewe and Derby; see P.S. Bagwell, *The Railway Men: The History of the National Union of Railwaymen* (1963), p.51.
72. PRO, RAIL 527/1901, Details of the Nine Hour Movement, 1881, records of the North-Eastern Railway Co.
73. *Royal Commission on Labour: Group B, Transport workers* (PP, 1892–93, XXXIII), Q.25, 975, evidence of George Findlay, General Manager of L & NWR.
74. Drummond, thesis, Chs.6 and 7 *Crewe Chronicle*, 9 Nov. 1881 and Chaloner, op. cit., Ch.VI.
75. *Crewe Chronicle*, 26 Oct. 1889.
76. Hames, op. cit., pp.68–75.
77. PRO, RAIL 410/264, Crewe and Locomotive Committee Minutes, Appendix 'A'.
78. PRO, RAIL 1025/102, Horwich Labourers' Arbitration, L & YR.
79. PRO, RAIL 1025/98, *Decision of the Industrial Court No.728* (July 1922), p.63.
80. Ibid.
81. PRO, RAIL 250/470, GWR Staff Matters.
82. PRO, RAIL 390/319, *Report on Utilisation of London and North-Eastern Railway Workshops*, 29 May 1923.

APPENDIX

TABLE 1

ESTABLISHMENT DATE OF RAILWAY COMPANY WORKSHOPS

Workshop	Railway Company	Opening Date	Locomotive Building	Closed
Shildon	Stockton & Darlington: North-Eastern Railway (1854)	1826/1830	Began 1867	1983 (Waggon works)
Darlington	S & D: NER	1850s	1863	1966
Gateshead	S & D: NER	1836		1919 Reopened 1932 Closed 1939
Middles-borough Stockton	S & D:NER North Hartlepool Co.	1840		
York (Locomotive & Carriage Works)	NER			
Doncaster	Great Northern Railway	1853		
Boston	GNR	1848		1853 Transferred to Doncaster
Miles Platting	Lancashire & Yorkshire			1887
Horwich	L & Y	1884		
Derby	Midland Counties: West Midland: Birmingham & Derby: Midland Co.	1840s 1844 1844		
Stoke-on-Trent	North–Staffordshire	1868		
Edgehill	Grand Junction Co.	1830		Transferred to Crewe 1843
Crewe	Grand Junction Railway Co. LNWR Co.	1843		
Wolver-hampton	GWR	1859		
Wolverton	London & Birmingham Co. L & NWR Co.	1845	1863	
Broadstone	GWR/Midland	1879		
Swindon	GWR	1842		
Stratford	Great Eastern	1851		
Bow	North London	1863		
Nine Elms	London & South Western	1843		1908

TABLE1continued

Workshop	Railway Company	Opening Date	Locomotive Building	Closed
Eastleigh	L & SWR	1887		
Brighton	London, Brighton & South Coast	1852		
Ashford	South-Eastern	1853		
Longhedge	London, Chatham & Dover	1869		
Cardiff	Taff Vale	1856		

Sources: Various PRO documents and James Lowe, *British Locomotive Builders* (Cambridge, 1975), p.10. Table: 'Output of Steam Locomotives by Main Railway Workshops'.

Table 2

MEMBERSHIP OF THE ASE AND SEM IN RAILWAY WORKS 1851–81

	1851	1871	1881
Darlington	?	61	98
Stockton	80	217	210
York	208	134	233
Doncaster	?	222	232
Derby	447	340	549
Crewe	517	797	1005
Wolverton	480	118	104
Stoke-on-Trent	–	79	89
Swindon	488	290	488
Stratford	28	?	229
Ashford	–	73	88
Brighton	42	?	?

Source: ASE Annual reports held at the Amalgamated Engineering Workers' headquarters and the SEM monthly reports held at the Bishopsgate Institute, London.

THE MEANINGS OF MANAGERIAL PREROGATIVE: INDUSTRIAL RELATIONS AND THE ORGANISATION OF WORK IN BRITISH ENGINEERING, 1880–1939

By ALAN McKINLAY and JONATHAN ZEITLIN

I

The last 15 years have witnessed an explosion of academic interest in the historical development of industrial work. The theoretical touchstone of this debate, Harry Braverman's *Labour and Monopoly Capitalism* (1974), depicted the evolution of industrial work as the progressive separation of conception and execution, in which machinery and Taylorism combined to wrest knowledge and control over work from an increasingly deskilled and enfeebled proletariat.[1] Braverman's argument has, however, come under increasingly severe criticism as historical and comparative studies have undermined the view that the evolution of specific labour processes can be deduced from an *a priori* model of capitalist development. The contingent nature of long run changes in work organisation has shifted attention from the refinement of teleological theories of industrial development to the search for an adequate method of studying change and continuity in work organisation. Particularly important in this respect is the insistence that the division of labour is shaped by the complex interaction between employer strategies, labour and product markets. In short, mass production is predicated upon mass consumption; the very possibility of deskilling hinges on the availability of predictable large scale demand for standard products which makes the deployment of highly specialised machinery commercially attractive. Confronted with shifting, heterogeneous demand or technological fluidity, employers, deterred by the inherent rigidities of volume production, will retain or develop flexible forms of work organisation based on adaptable machinery operated by workers capable of working efficiently without detailed task specification.[2] A final determinant of sectoral and national diversity is the mediation of economic relationships by the development of industrial relations institutions, the outcomes of conflicts between unions and employers and even between different work groups.[3]

Historical analysis of changing industrial relations and work organisation in engineering has meshed with Braverman's analysis to produce an influential account in which deskilling played a central role in managerial strategies. In brief, confronted with increased competition in international markets, engineering employers responded by introducing new automatic machine tools that dispensed with much of the craft skills, which had formed the historic power base of the industry's skilled workforce.[4] The engineering employers' determined challenge to the craftsmen's workplace power, which reached unprecedented heights in the lock-outs of 1897–98 and 1922, also had profound social and political effects. By narrowing skill and earnings differentials within the industrial workforce such changes in work organisation constituted the necessary prelude to industrial rather than sectional trade unionism and a wider class awareness which found its most popular political expression in the Labour Party.[5] Our purpose in this article is to challenge a vital element of this interpretation, specifically, that British engineering employers pursued a collective strategy designed fundamentally to transform the nature of work.

A case study of engineering, with its two lock-outs over the definition of managerial prerogative in 1897–98 and 1922, offers an empirical test of how employers understood and articulated their individual and collective interests. Equally important, engineering affords us an opportunity to examine how employers used their painfully won power and authority both in labour relations and work organisation. The engineering employers' collective demand for 'managerial functions' was not a simple, automatic expression of their class interest. What is apparent in engineering is not the singularity and clarity of employers' strategic visions and ideology but the diversity and deep ambiguity which underlay demands for 'managerial prerogative'. Indeed, we shall argue that this ambiguity was a central constitutive element in the formation of the Engineering Employers' Federation (EEF).

Just as the powerful resonance of the abstract principle of managerial prerogative masked considerable diversity in definition so the EEF was subject to constant internal strains. In large part, this reflected the extreme heterogeneity of the engineering industry which comprised a series of distinct but overlapping sectors linked by a common set of metalworking processes and associated manual skills. Before 1914 the most important sectors produced a variety of capital goods with vehicles and electrical engineering assuming an increasing share of total output, particularly after 1918. Each sector was exposed to significantly different market conditions with variations in profitability, the extent of competition and market stability.[6] Sectoral diversity was overlaid by regional specialisation, often reinforced by contractual and familial ties between firms, resulting in a potent localism expressed through the Federation's constituent area associations.

Such cross-cutting pressures proved formidable barriers to sustained national employer cohesion with recurring crises of central authority within the Federation. Despite repeated attempts, the EEF's leaders proved unable to win the engineering unions' consent to the transformation of the industry's procedural agreement into a comprehensive national settlement governing wages and working conditions, in part because of resistance from their own members to proposed concessions. At the same time, moreover, such internal divisions within the Federation left little scope for unilateral amplification of managerial prerogative into a substantive code specifying machine manning arrangements, training methods or payment systems for the industry as a whole. Hence, despite their overwhelming victories in 1898 and 1922 engineering employers made limited progress in reshaping work organisation while their continued dependence on skilled labour left them vulnerable to craft militancy revived by tight labour markets.

II

For four decades after 1850 an implicit accommodation structured relations between engineering employers and their skilled workers. The basis of this accommodation was British economic supremacy and the assimilation of technical innovation within a broadly stable division of labour based on craft labour. After mid-century, slow-growing international markets replaced the previously expansive domestic market as the mainstay of engineering demand. This shift in the focus of the industry's product market was associated with a move toward less standardised production. In turn, this consolidated the vital role of skilled labour as productive flexibility became an essential of sustained competitive advantage. The long period of relatively stagnant demand for engineering products ushered in by the Great Depression of the 1870s shifted the balance between price competitiveness and flexibility. Cost pressures stimulated employer experimentation with methods of cheapening and intensifying skilled labour within existing craft based work processes. As a result, the simpler, mechanised tasks which comprised the base of the hierarchy of skilled work were allocated to semi-skilled 'handymen' and boys, while apprentices were recruited in ever greater numbers and increasingly confined to repetition work at the expense of their technical training. Piecework, intensive supervision and systematic overtime also became common methods of undercutting standard wage rates and wringing increased output from skilled engineers on unchanged equipment. This assault on craft regulation eroded the major achievements of engineering trade unionism, the control of apprentice numbers and the establishment of the standard working day and common district wage rates.[7]

The continued centrality of craft workers in engineering ensured that employer production strategies were contested by the craft societies over the course of the trade cycle with recurrent clashes over wages, hours and working conditions. Craft militancy intensified during the trade recovery of the late 1880s and a process of regional leapfrogging was sustained by informal union co-ordinating committees. In 1893 a sharp downturn in trade focused union militancy on limiting unemployment by reducing working time. Only deepening recession in 1895 halted the national campaign for an eight-hour day but not before significant employers had acceded to union demands.[8] Growing industrial relations tension was given a novel dimension with the slow diffusion of American machine tools throughout British manufacturing following their successful introduction in the cycle industry. While the practical impact of turret and capstan lathes, milling and grinding machines and precision gauges was limited outside the nascent mass production cycle industry, the productive potential of these technical innovations called into question the position of skilled craftsmen within the division of labour.[9] The uneven wave of mechanisation which began in the early 1890s paralleled the increasing discord within the industry until the separate but related issues of managerial authority and work rationalisation became fused as craftsmen endeavoured to re-establish control over existing equipment and extend craft regulation to cover new techniques.

For almost a decade efforts to create a national federation of engineering employers had foundered on the varying tempos of industrial relations in different manufacturing sectors. After 1890, craftsmen's struggles to rebuild traditional job controls and extend these principles to new mechanised techniques provided engineering employers with a shared focus on the 'machine question'. The double-edged nature of the 'machine question', a term embracing employer hostility to resurrected craft controls and their insistence on a free hand in the deployment of novel machinery, placed the issue high on the managerial agenda. If the locality fixed the boundaries to employer co-ordination in the decade before 1896 then there was significant progress in the employers' tactical awareness. In reply to the union strategy of enforcing general demands by picking off particular companies in turn, the Belfast, Clyde and North-East Coast employers developed the tactic of escalating disputes at a single firm into regional confrontations by locking out union members in stages of 25 per cent per week. If the widespread experience of different facets of craft militancy and the success of regional concerted action were undoubtedly important, then the universal nature of the eight-hour demand was the final, compelling stimulus behind the creation of a national employers' federation in 1896, the Engineering Employers' Federation.[10]

Ultimately, the national lock-out was triggered not by the 'machine question' but by the resumption of the movement for the eight-hour day in London, an area whose weak employers' association had initially remained outside the EEF. Employer resolve rapidly collapsed in the face of union pressure and in a desperate bid to staunch the flow of defeats the London association hastily joined the EEF in June 1897. Determined to prevent the leapfrogging process so successfully deployed by the union in previous disputes, the EEF immediately threatened to lock-out 25 per cent of all ASE men in federated firms per week until the shorter hours demand was withdrawn. By deliberately recasting the terms of engagement in industrial conflict in this manner the employers could inflict serious damage on union funds while allowing member firms to maintain production during a period of buoyant demand. Resistance to the eight-hour day was favourable ground on which to mobilise the new federation's membership drawn from diverse sectors and districts:

reduced working time would reduce productivity, increase costs and threaten the competitive position of firms across the industry as a whole.

The EEF had laid elaborate plans for the confrontation, including a strike levy on member firms, the establishment of a benefit society to break the ties between supervisors and the craft unions, a supply of blackleg labour and a national 'enquiry note' system to ensure the effectiveness of the lock-out. Nevertheless, there were significant gaps in employer solidarity with notable abstentions and defections from Federation membership among textile machinery manufacturers, marine engineers and the great railway workshops.[11] But the chinks in the employers' armour were minor compared to the glaring weaknesses the lock-out exposed in the ASE. The ASE, despite mushrooming membership growth, was ill-prepared for a full scale confrontation. The ASE had organised fewer than half the skilled engineers in the industry and none of the burgeoning legions of handymen capable of operating the new machine tools. Equally, the ASE's fierce defence of the boundaries of the engineer's trade had isolated the union from the other great craft societies which remained aloof from the dispute.[12]

The cost of financing the six-month dispute brought the ASE to the verge of bankruptcy and forced its leaders to sue for peace. The Terms of Settlement accepted by ASE members in January 1898 conceded a legitimate role for collective bargaining over wages in return for a sweeping recognition of managerial prerogatives in other spheres. The ASE acknowledged the employers' right to hire non-unionists, to institute piecework systems at prices agreed with the individual worker, to demand up to forty hours' overtime per man each month, to pay non-unionists at individual rates, to employ as many apprentices as they chose, and to place any suitable worker on any machine at a mutually agreed rate. The 1898 Settlement struck at the core of craft regulation, the nexus of practices which skilled engineers sought to impose unilaterally as a condition of their employment. Finally, the Terms of Settlement established a novel disputes procedure which enshrined the employers' corporate strategy of elevating any dispute from the firm to the regional and, ultimately, the national level: henceforth the ASE could not sanction any strike until it had gone through a national conference between the union executive and the EEF.[13] These procedural arrangements were designed to discourage local resistance on questions of principle by forcing the ASE executive to discipline its members through the constant threat of a renewed national lock-out.

The EEF's victory in 1898 inaugurated an employer dominated national collective bargaining system. Yet the internal frictions generated within the EEF's ranks by the increasingly integrated bargaining structure indicate deep and continuing ambiguities in the meaning of 'managerial prerogative'. Above all, as custodian of engineering employers' collective interest, the EEF had to strike the balance between concession and coercion which would preserve the 1898 Settlement with minimal damage to the Federation's internal cohesion. The Federation's difficulties in formulating an acceptable national strategy were heightened by the revival of union organisation and growing governmental intolerance of employer unilateralism, particularly during the Liberal administrations of 1906–14.[14]

The reassertion of managerial prerogatives in 1897–98 was not the prelude to the wholesale transformation of work organisation in engineering. Product market constraints continued to limit the commercial appeal and practicality of rationalisation. The majority of British engineering products continued to be manufactured in comparatively small batches using flexible methods of production. Even in buoyant sectors dominated by large firms producing relatively standardised goods such as cycles, motors and electrical engineering where rationalisation progressed furthest, the limited scope of the domestic market discouraged a complete transition to mass production. In traditional sectors whose products lent themselves to standardisation, particularly armaments, and textile and agricultural machinery, fragmented demand compelled even specialised firms utilising standard designs to maintain an extremely wide product range. At most, British engineering was an uneasy hybrid poised between craft and mass production. More often, however, such nuances were notable only by their absence. New machine tools were primarily used to increase the quality rather than the volume of final products whose designs were dictated by customer specifications with little regard to the long-term economies of scale possible though volume production. The majority of EEF member firms' main concern was with loosening craft regulation, continuing with work intensification strategies firmly established before the lock-out, rather than the pursuit of pervasive deskilling.[15]

The employers' dependence on the inventiveness of skilled labour to cope with product variability enabled the ASE quickly to rebuild its organisation. The revitalisation of grassroots trade unionism, including the slow emergence of the shop steward as a central figure in industrial politics, was associated with a guerrilla struggle over job controls. The EEF's response to bursts of localised craft militancy was either to threaten the ASE with a national confrontation or, more commonly, to use informal pressure on the union leadership while financially supporting the affected firm. While the EEF's strategy successfully contained local issues its effectiveness was dependent upon maintaining the credibility of the disputes procedure, even when decisions were unfavourable to particular employers. Between 1900 and 1907 the Federation made significant concessions on substantive issues such as piece rate fixing, overtime limits and the displacement of skilled workers by machines to confirm the ASE's voluntary adherence to the Terms of Settlement. But the EEF refused amendments which would compromise the underlying principles of managerial prerogative, insisting that the disputes procedure remained retrospective, triggered only after a managerial innovation.[16] An important reason for the EEF's tactical flexibility was that its collective strength could only

be fully mobilised if a fundamental tenet of managerial prerogative
was threatened.[17] As the disputes procedure gradually assimilated wage
questions as well as issues of principle the leaderships of both the EEF
and the ASE experienced increasing difficulty in satisfying the disparate
demands of their respective memberships. While the EEF leadership
managed to maintain its authority its union counterpart suffered severe
difficulties in restraining local militancy stimulated by growing skilled
labour shortages in the three years before 1914. In this period, the union
began to win significant victories across a broad range of issues, from
machine manning and apprenticeship to wages and payment systems.
This process culminated in the ASE's unilateral termination of the 1898
settlement and the renewal of its demand for 48-hour week, an offensive
tempered only by the union's grudging acceptance of an interim disputes
procedure which made no reference to managerial prerogatives.

Conscious of the internal and external obstacles to another national
lock-out, the EEF leadership sought a peaceful resolution of the crisis,
offering a variety of concessions including reduced working hours in
exchange for adherence to revised Terms of Settlement. At the same
time, however, the Federation also warned the ASE executive against
the risks of unilateral action in the districts on sensitive issues such as the
closed shop. On the eve of the Great War the edifice of managerial and
procedural hegemony constructed in 1897–98 had crumbled. It remained
an open question whether another national trial of strength would be the
outcome or if the situation could be resolved through negotiation.[18]

III

The history of the engineering industry during the First World War
has been narrated at length elsewhere, and it is our intention simply
to highlight those aspects of wartime developments relevant to the
prolonged struggle to define managerial prerogative. Far from being
the pliant tool of industrial capital the wartime state proved peculiarly
immune to business influence, even where manufacturers were seconded
as advisers to the war departments. The state's first priority was to ensure
the flow of munitions and manpower necessary for military victory, a
priority which relegated commercial considerations to the margins of
policy making. By contrast, the representation of organised labour at
all levels of the state bureaucracy was explicitly geared to winning labour
support for government policy. The framework of wartime labour policy
was established by the 1915 Treasury Agreement, a bilateral compact
between Lloyd George and the unions which suspended the right to
strike in return for legal guarantees of the full restoration of pre-war
work practices.[19]

The exclusion of employers from industrial legislation at the national
level was paralleled in the regions by the government's susceptibility to
labour pressure. For many of the EEF's regional associations even the
wartime legal limitations on labour mobility, job controls and defensive

practices were insufficient to redress the balance of power in their favour. Chronic shortages of skilled labour and the consequent earnings drift completely undermined the established mechanisms of employer cohesion in local labour markets. This collapse of employer solidarity increased their frustration both at the perceived partiality of the state and at the EEF's inability to prevent these reverses. Indeed, by 1916 such was the disaffection of employers in areas where the industrial situation was most acute that the EEF seemed on the verge of disintegration. Only a reversal of the Federation's conciliatory labour policy and an increased voice for the most restive association maintained the integrity of the EEF as a national organisation.[20]

Throughout the war engineering employers experienced significant incursions into managerial prerogatives not only from shop stewards on the factory floor but also from legislative limitations on their power to rebuff such challenges. Even legal provisions designed to control labour were inherently double-edged, in that through tripartite tribunals employer inefficiencies could be used by the unions to temper managerial authority. It was with evident relief that the employers greeted the final demise of wartime labour legislation in 1921, 'the severing of the last tentacle of the octopus of Government control which gripped industry and employers and employed alike during the past six years'.[21]

Just as the experience of the Great War confirmed British employers' mistrust of state involvement in industry so it reinforced their established production strategies. The insatiable demand for standardised munitions products temporarily released metal manufacturers from the limits to rationalisation imposed by the variegated demands of their established markets. Worried by the inefficiency and inflexibility of mass production engineering employers overwhelmingly rejected Taylorism as inappropriate for the high-quality, small-batch production which again dominated British engineering after the Armistice.[22]

While EEF membership had doubled between 1914–18 the Federation's leadership faced the daunting prospect of rebuilding employer solidarity and central authority after the divisive traumas of the Great War. Internal surveys revealed the extent of the disarray within the EEF. Beneath the unanimous adherence to the abstract principle of managerial prerogative, potentially crippling discrepancies were apparent over a broad spectrum of vital issues, from the future basis of wage determination and the length of the working day to the acceptability of shop committees. A number of associations also expressed their doubts about the possibility of restoring untrammeled managerial freedom on key questions such as payment systems, overtime, training and the closed shop. Under these circumstances, concluded Allan Smith, the Federation's chairman, employers' collective interests could only be safeguarded through a bold national strategy aimed at reaching a durable accommodation with organised labour even at the price of substantial reductions in hours and a greater degree of joint regulation over wages and working conditions.[23]

At the same time, however, Smith sought to reconstruct the Federation's capacity for collective action by internal reforms to increase recruitment and coordinate bargaining strategy across districts and by forging closer links with other employers' organisations outside engineering.[24] The pursuit of Smith's 'national programme' dominated the EEF's bargaining strategy in the immediate post-war years. Faced with mounting industrial unrest in the wake of the armistice, the Federation conceded a 47-hour week in November 1918 in exchange for general promises by the trade union leaders to promote maximum output and negotiate seriously on the introduction of payment by results.[25] But these promises proved virtually unenforceable in 1919–20 as district committees and shop stewards broke free from central union control, and engineering employers were thrown onto the defensive by unilateral restrictions on machine manning, payment systems, apprenticeship ratios and overtime working. Throughout this period, however, Smith and the EEF leaders maintained a cautious posture, urging employers to exercise 'the utmost discretion and tact' and afford 'workpeople the opportunity of raising any question in a constitutional way'.[26] Only when confronted with official union support for unilateral action did they resort to the lock-out threat, as in the case of the electricians' demand for the closed shop for foremen in 1920.[27]

The central focus of Federation strategy, by contrast, was directed to protracted negotiations with union executives – above all the AEU – for a comprehensive national agreement on wages procedure and working conditions which would resolve the full range of disputed issues. Smith himself was prepared to offer far-reaching concessions such as recognised bargaining rights for apprentices and a national grading system for semi-skilled labour in return for union acceptance of payment by results and greater flexibility in machine manning, and influential figures within the AEU executive were sympathetic to the general thrust of these proposals.[28] The high water mark of this campaign for the 'national programme' was the Overtime and Night Shift Agreement of September 1920 which levelled up rates and conditions across districts, an agreement pushed through by Smith in hopes of unblocking negotiations on wider issues and putting an end to local embargoes on overtime.[29]

But the EEF's conciliatory strategy ran into growing opposition from disgruntled regional associations experiencing little relief from localised militancy and concerned about the costs of proposed concessions. These grievances sharpened during 1920 as the post-war boom burst and recession spread unevenly across engineering. The worst-hit sectors began to clamour for immediate wage cuts, while the Overtime and Night Shift Agreement in particular sparked bitter resentment from those regions facing sharply increased rates. All of Smith's authority and diplomatic skills were required to persuade dissident associations to adopt 'a broad national standpoint' for the moment, but the scope for further compromises with the union had clearly been narrowed.[30] Under such pressures, the Federation's commitment to a bargained settlement could only be sustained if union leaders demonstrated their ability to deliver the *quid pro quo* of local compliance with national agreements. As unemployment began to bite more deeply, however, the conciliatory faction within the AEU executive itself lost ground to the defenders of unilateral craft restrictions. Thus in December 1920, the union threw its official weight behind the claim that district committees could maintain their overtime embargoes despite the provisions of the Overtime and Night Shift Agreement which fixed a limit of 30 hours per man per month.[31] Given the unpopularity of this agreement among engineering employers, the AEU's position struck at the heart of Smith's attempt to establish a mutually acceptable framework for industrial relations through national negotiations with union officials. In early 1921, therefore, the EEF threatened to dismiss anyone refusing to work overtime up to the agreed limits and lock out the AEU if it struck in their defence.[32]

From that point onwards, Smith and his colleagues appear to have decide that the weakness of central authority within the unions now required a unilateral reassertion of managerial prerogatives. But if the collapse of the post-war boom eliminated the gross disparities between different sectors of engineering, the shift in economic circumstances did not automatically swing employer opinion behind a confrontation with the unions over these issues. Recession did, however, galvanise the EEF to press for an immediate rollback of wage advances granted between 1917 and 1920. Under heavy pressure from the employers, the unions conceded a staged reduction in July 1921, despite an adverse vote of their members, but by the autumn the EEF was demanding further cuts of 26s. 6d. per week. Smith and the Federation leaders used this crucial period to mobilise support among their members for a broad campaign to extract a formal recognition of managerial prerogatives from the unions and impose a new procedural arrangement on the industry. For many employers, however, the EEF's focus on questions of abstract principle represented an unwelcome distraction from the burning need for a drastic reduction in wage costs to restore their international competitiveness. Union restrictions in any case had largely evaporated as the recession deepened, and even the AEU's overtime embargoes had become more symbolic than real. Hence the Federation's proposals to extend the threatened lock-out from overtime to managerial prerogatives in April 1921 met with a distinctly ambivalent response in many districts.[33]

But the downward spiral of industrial demand progressively diminished the potential costs of a lock-out to the employers, while the strategic rigidity of the AEU enhanced the ideological attractiveness of a formal restoration of managerial prerogatives. With union funds depleted by heavy employment, by November 1921 the AEU executive felt compelled to accept the EEF's interpretation of the overtime agreement and the employers' right to initiate changes in the workplace pending the conclusion of the disputes procedure, but the proposed memorandum on managerial functions was rejected by a membership ballot. At this point, employer opinion swung decisively behind the Federation's confrontational stance, and Smith was even able to extend the lock-out threat to all other unions in the industry unless they too signed the disputed memorandum. Even more than in 1897, however, the demand for managerial prerogatives articulated in 1922 encompassed a host of divergent production and labour strategies. If the engineering employers now appeared to speak with a single voice, this reflected no singularity of purpose: collective strength was deployed to protect the autonomy of individual firms, not to advance a collective project of work rationalisation.

From the beginning, the 1922 lock-out was more comprehensive than that of 1897–98; from March all AEU members refusing to sign the contentious document were barred from federated factories, and 51 other unions were thrown onto the streets for the same reason in May. A bitter war of attrition lasting over three months finally exhausted the unions' finances and morale. Driven to insolvency the AEU was a spent force, its capacity for national action decisively shattered.[34] Unlike 1898 the EEF's victory was complete; all engineering unions had been brought within the ambit of a uniform national bargaining system and compelled to acknowledge the legitimacy of managerial prerogatives. For the EEF, the central merit of the 1922 Settlement was that it extended the principles laid down in 1898, namely, that 'each stage of the procedure removed the question one stage further from the contending parties'.[35] The centripetal nature of the bargaining system was intended to increase the leverage of union executives over local and workshop representatives as a further check on grassroots incursions into managerial authority.

For more than a decade after 1922 the engineering union was all but impotent at the national, regional and workshop levels. Unlike the 1898–1914 period when grassroots activism had revived the ASE, in the decade after 1922 activism within the demoralised, declining union turned inwards towards factionalism.[36] Despite their new legitimacy in bargaining procedures shop stewards dwindled not only in numbers but also in the scope of their concerns. Where they retained a significant presence, shop stewards focused almost exclusively on the grievances of highly skilled engineers whose experience and versatility gave them a greater degree of employment security. Cuts in wages and lowered working conditions negotiated at the national level were not, therefore, compensated by collective bargaining at factory level. This pattern reflected the logic of the 1898 and 1922 Settlement: the use of collective might to enhance the discretionary power of the particular employer in substantive issues. As a result, an increased centralisation of wage bargaining was parallelled by ever greater diversity in other areas, such as training, payment systems and machine manning.

Throughout this period Smith and other EEF officials sought to instil a greater strategic awareness among its members, but without the external threat of union power their leverage was sharply diminished. Federation initiatives on key issues such as training and grading therefore foundered on the limited time horizons imposed on manufacturers by depressed trade and their ability to cut production costs without recourse to industry-wide measures. As Smith warned, however, this strategic 'shortsightedness', would have serious consequences for labour supply and industrial relations when trade eventually improved.[37]

In heavy engineering, job controls were undermined by the progressive individualisation of shopfloor bargaining. But weak demand provided little incentive for either capital or organisational investment. In areas such as Clydeside, although a significant minority of firms retained time work the use of payment by results rapidly increased. There was, however, no concerted movement towards deskilling and the bureaucratisation of factory authority structures. On the contrary, an 'expert adviser' hired by the Clyde association to popularise Taylorist ideas resigned after less than a year completely disheartened by his lack of success.[38] Incentive payment systems were primarily used by craft foremen to manipulate existing social and technical gradations within the engineering workforce, to blur still further the distinction between 'skilled' and 'non-skilled' work. Skill became an increasingly fluid concept dependent upon the balance of forces in a given locality and even the particular factory rather than simply ascribed by the completion, or otherwise, of an apprenticeship.

Even in the car industry product market conditions inhibited the diffusion of Fordist techniques. In the context of a highly fragmented, quasi-luxury market further complicated by seasonal fluctuations, employers similarly rejected mass production as inappropriate. Rather than a wholesale movement towards direct control over the labour process, British car firms developed a wide variety of production regimes in which flexibility and maximising effort through tightly controlled piecework systems were key features. Within this framework management willingly ceded a high degree of autonomy to production workers in task performance to maximise flexibility while supervisory power was effectively unchecked in a highly insecure and poorly unionised industry.[39] In short, before 1939 work organisation in engineering as a whole was characterised by strained continuity rather than dramatic change.

The beginning of rearmament in 1935 marked the beginning of a rapid, but uneven recovery for engineering. A tightening labour market for skilled labour was the backdrop to rejuvenation of engineering trade unionism. An outstanding feature of the resurgence of workplace collective bargaining was that its first target was the elimination of the accumulated excesses of managerial authority which built up unchecked during the depression. Initially, shopfloor activists won symbolic victories such as the right to smoke at work but the challenge to managerial authority soon encompassed the collective regulation of payment systems, the allocation of short time and the demand for the closed shop.[40] All such demands contravened the letter and spirit of employer unilateralism enshrined in the 1922 Settlement. In turn, the challenge to employer authority at factory level placed an intolerable burden on the industry's cumbersome disputes procedure, compelling the EEF to adopt a more flexible, conciliatory stance.[41] The most dramatic reversal suffered by the employers was the success of the 1937 apprentices' strikes which forced the EEF to accept union negotiation of apprentice wages and conditions for the first time in its history.[42] As the EEF had predicted, the employers' failure to devise common policies towards labour market regulation during the period when they dominated industrial relations left them vulnerable to a revival of craft militancy. Without a framework of substantive protocols to define the limits of managerial prerogatives in practice the employers' historic claim for absolute authority proved impossible to sustain in the long term.

IV

The two lock-outs which punctuated the history of British engineering between 1880 and 1939 were the product of long-term economic pressures and specific circumstances which permitted the employers to coalesce around the demand for managerial freedom. If 1897–98 represented a watershed moment in the employers' tactical awareness through their use of a rolling lock-out then this did not mark the beginning of a unified collective strategy. Rather, the EEF remained an extremely hesitant organisation in which solidarity could be mobilised only on the most fundamental issues. The tensions within the Federation were evident even during the prelude to the 1922 dispute when widespread depression which reduced the cost of conflict to a minimum failed to convince all federated firms of the necessity or wisdom of confrontation. Once the formal sway of managerial prerogatives had been restored, moreover, strategic immobilism became the price for continued cohesion within an organisation unable to pursue broader definitions of employers' collective interests than the defence of the rights of individual firms.

If exploring the political dimension of employer organisation dispenses with assumptions that the EEF was an unitary expression of class interests then the trajectory of work organisation in engineering after the two lock-outs undermines teleological models of industrial development. A shifting combination of product market constraints, deeply embedded craft unionism and employer reluctance to commit substantial capital or organisational investment severely limited the pace of change in work organisation. The continued centrality of skilled workers within the division of labour was the basis of the resurgence of workplace militancy after 1935 which derived much of its impetus from a widespread desire to temper iniquitous managerial practices accumulated during the depression.

Centre for Business History in Scotland,
University of Glasgow
Birkbeck College, University of London

NOTES

For convenience we refer to the Engineering Employers' Federation throughout this article as the organisation has changed its name several times. This article draws to a small extent on material which will also appear in a different context in S. Tolliday and J. Zeitlin (eds.), *The Power to Manage: Employers and Industrial Relations in Comparative-Historical Perspective* (forthcoming).

1. H. Braverman, *Labor and Monopoly Capitalism* (New York, 1974). For related but more sophisticated reformulations of this general approach, see, inter alia, M. Burawoy, *The Politics of Production*, (London, 1985); A. Friedman, *Industry and Labour* (London, 1977); D. Gordon, R. Edwards and M. Reich, *Segmented Work, Divided Workers* (Cambridge, 1982).
2. For overviews of these criticisms, see S. Wood (ed.), *The Degradation of Work? Skill, Deskilling and the Labour Process* (London, 1982); D. Knights, H. Willmott and D. Collinson (eds.), *Job Redesign: Critical Perspectives on the Labour Process* (Aldershot, 1985); and J. Zeitlin, 'Social Theory and the History of Work', *Social History*, Vol.8, No.3 (1983), pp.365–74.
3. J. Zeitlin, 'From Labour History to the History of Industrial Relations', *Economic History Review*, Vol.XL, No.2 (1987), pp.159–84.
4. K. Burgess, *The Challenge of Labour* (London, 1980); R.Q. Gray, *The Labour Aristocracy in Victorian Edinburgh* (Oxford, 1976); J. Storey, *Managerial Prerogative and the Question of Control* (London, 1983).
5. J. Hinton, *The First Shop Stewards' Movement* (London, 1973); J.B. Jeffreys, *The Story of the Engineers* (London, 1946); R. McKibbin, 'Why was there no Marxism in Great Britain?', *English Historical Review*, No.99 (1984), pp.297, 331.
6. S.B. Saul, 'The Market and the Development of the Mechanical Engineering Industries in Britain, 1760–1914', *Economic History Review*, Vol.20, No.2 (1967), pp.110–30; and *idem.*, 'Engineering', in D.H. Aldcroft (ed.), *The Development of British Industry and Foreign Competition, 1875–1914* (London, 1968), pp.186–237; R. Floud, *The British Machine Tool Industry, 1850–1914* (Cambridge, 1976).
7. K. Burgess, *The Origins of British Industrial Relations* (London, 1975), pp.1–85; J. Zeitlin, 'Engineers and Compositors: A Comparison', in R. Harrison and J. Zeitlin (eds.), *Divisions of Labour: Skilled Workers in Nineteenth Century Britain* (Brighton, 1985), pp.198–206; W. Knox, 'Apprenticeship and Deskilling in Britain', *International Review of Social History*, Vol.XXXI (1986), pp.172–5.
8. B.C.M Weekes, 'The Amalgamated Society of Engineers, 1880–1914', Ph.D thesis, University of Warwick, 1970, pp.61–80; E. Wigham, *The Power to Manage* (London, 1973), pp.123–4.
9. S.B. Saul, 'The American Impact on British Industry, 1895–1914', *Business History*, Vol.III, No.1 (1960), pp.19–38; see also the sources cited in note 6.
10. J. Zeitlin, 'The Labour Strategies of British Engineering Employers, 1890–1922', in H. Gospel and C. Litter (eds.), *Managerial Strategies and Industrial Relations* (London, 1983), pp.26–33; *idem*, 'Lt.–Col. Henry Clement Swinerton Dyer', in D. Jeremy (ed.), *The Dictionary of Business Biography* Vol.II (London, 1984), pp.217–21; Wigham, op. cit., pp.20–42.
11. EEF, *List of the Federated Engineering and Shipbuilding Employers who Resisted the Demand for a 48 Hours Working Week* (London, 1898); 'Railway Companies and the 48 Hours Demand, 1897', EEF Archives, microfilm H(10)1; Wigham, op. cit., pp.47–9.
12. Zeitlin, 'Labour Strategies', op. cit., pp.33–4, and the sources cited therein.
13. Wigham, op. cit., pp.54–62; H.A. Clegg, A. Fox and A. Thompson, *A History of British Trade Unions since 1889*, Vol.1 (Oxford, 1964), pp.161–7.
14. For fears of government intervention as a constraint on EEF strategy after 1906, see

A. Smith, 'Present Procedure in Dealing with Wages Questions' (n.d., 1908), EEF C(4)11; and 'Circular Letter to Local Associations on Wages Questions', 30 April 1913, EEF W(2)2.

15. Zeitlin, 'Labour Strategies', op. cit., pp.35–45; *idem.*, 'Between Flexibility and Mass Production: Product, Production and Labour Strategies in British Engineering, 1880–1939', unpublished paper presented to the 'International Working Group on Historical Alternatives to Mass Production', Lyon, 24–6 June 1988.

16. *Verbatim Report of Conferences between the EEF and the ASE, SEMS and UMWA, December–May 1900;* transcripts of further conferences re amendments to the Terms of Settlement, 1906–7, EEF A(2)5–9.

17. See, for example, the comments of A.P. Henderson, the EEF's Executive Chairman: 'It would be a very difficult thing to get the Federation lined up against the ASE . . . We need a very strong case to put before the Federation before we will get them to be as prepared to go into the sacrifice as they did on the previous occasion'. Transcript of a Special Meeting of the Executive Board, 10 July 1906, EEF H(4)4.

18. Transcripts of conferences with the ASE and other unions on disputes procedure and Terms of Agreement, February-April 1914, EEF A(4)7 and 11; memoranda and circular letters on the reduction of working hours, 1913–14, EEF H(1); A. Smith to W. Weir, 22 April 1914, EEF E(1)29; EEF Conference Committee Minutes, 9–10 July 1914; J.R. Richmond (Weirs), *Some Aspects of Labour and its Claims in the Engineering Industry, presidential address to Glasgow University Engineering Society, (1916–1917)*, pp.5–7.

19. A. Reid, 'Dilution, Trade Unionism and the State in Britain during the First World War', in S. Tolliday and J. Zeitlin (eds.), *Shopfloor Bargaining and the State* (Cambridge, 1985), pp.60–66; J. Turner, 'The Politics of "Organised Business" in the First World War', in J. Turner (ed.), *Businessmen and Politics* (London, 1984), pp.39–43.

20. Memoranda, correspondence and meetings of Clyde employers, 1915, EEF W(4)5–6; J.R. Richmond to A.P. Henderson, 12 Aug. 1916, and J.E. Thorneycroft to A. Smith, 17 Aug. 1916, EEF C(2)5; EEF Emergency Committee Minutes, 25 Aug., 15 Sept. and 24 Nov. 1916. For a fuller account, see Wigham, op. cit., pp.86–97; and J. Zeitlin, 'The Internal Politics of Employer Organization: The Engineering Employers' Federation, 1896–1939', in S. Tolliday and J. Zeitlin (eds.), *The Power to Manage? Employers and Industrial Relations in Comparative – Historical Perspective* (forthcoming, London, 1989).

21. *Glasgow Herald*, 12 April, 1921, cited in G. Rubin, *War, Law, and Labour* (Oxford, 1987), p.242.

22. C. More, *Skill and the English Working Class, 1870–1914* (London, 1980), p.32; A. McKinlay, 'Employers and Skilled Workers in the Inter-War Depression: Engineering and Shipbuilding on Clydeside, 1919–1939', D. Phil. thesis, Oxford, 1986, pp.64–6.

23. EEF, 'Memorandum on Post-War Industrial Problems', and 'Tabulation of Replies from Local Associations', September 1916, EEF I(1)7; Management Committee Report No.56, 28 Aug. 1917, precis of responses from local associations to the Whitley Report, I(1)9; 'Post-War Industrial Problems', interim report by special sub-committee, 21 Jan. 1918, EEF I(1)12; A. Smith to V. Caillard, 24 Sept. 1918, EEF S(4)19; Smith to J. Barr, 22 Oct. 1918, EEF C(6) 1918.

24. On EEF internal reforms, see Management Committee Minutes, 31 Aug. 1917; and A.J. McIvor, 'Employers' Associations and Industrial Relations in Lancashire', Ph.D thesis, Manchester, 1983, pp.372–6. For the EEF's relations with other employers' organisations, see Turner, op. cit.; T. Rodgers, 'Work and Welfare: The National Confederation of Employers' Organisations and the Unemployment Question, 1919–1936', Ph.D. thesis, Edinburgh, 1981, pp.14–25; EEF C(2)2, C(8)1–2, I(1)12 and S(3)6.

25. Transcripts of conferences between the EEF, the Shipbuilding Employers' Federation and various trade unions, Oct.–Nov. 1918, EEF H(3)17.

26. 'Industrial Unrest', EEF circular letter to local associations, 11 Aug. 1919.

27. Wigham, op. cit., pp.114–15; J. Melling, 'Employers and the Rise of Supervisory

Unionism', in C.J. Wrigley (ed.), *A History of British Industrial Relations, Vol.II; 1914–39* (Brighton, 1986), pp.254–6.

28. The evolution of the Federation's bargaining position and the union response can be followed in the multi-volume transcripts of the national negotiations on working conditions 1919–24 in the EEF collection at the Modern Records Centre, University of Warwick, MSS. 237/1/13/1 and 237/1/12/4–13. The clearest accounts of Smith's overall strategy appear in his speeches to the London and District Engineering Employers' Association, 17 Dec. 1918, and the North-West Engineering Trades Employers' Association (NWETEA), 25 Jan. 1921, EEF G(1)7 and 8. For a fuller analysis, see J. Zeitlin, *The Triumph of Adversarial Bargaining: Industrial Relations in British Engineering, 1880–1939* (Oxford, forthcoming).

29. Transcript of a special conference between the EEF and engineering trade unions, 29–30 Sept. 1920.

30. For dissent by leading employers to Smith's policies, see Birmingham and District Engineering Employers' Associations to EEF 16 Aug. 1919, EEF C(8)2; 'Replies from Associations to Circular Letter of 1 Oct. 1920 *re* Overtime and Night Shift Agreement'. EEF W(9)4. App. 26; letters to Smith from Sir H. Spencer (2 and 31 Dec. 1920), P.W. Robson (15 and 23 Dec. 1920), J.R. Richmond (21 Dec. 1920), all in C(6)1920; and transcript of a general meeting of the NWETEA, 25 Jan. 1921, from which the quotation is taken.

31. AEU Executive Council Minutes, 31 Aug., 6 and 28 Sept., 9 and 10 Oct., 22 and 24 Nov., 21–23 Dec. 1920.

32. Transcript of a special conference between the EEF and the AEU, 12–13 Jan. 1921; EEF Management Committee Minutes, 17 and 25 Feb. 1921.

33. N.W.E.T.E.A., Executive Committee Minutes, 19 April 1921; F. Robson to Smith, 22 May and 15 Sept. 1921, EEF C(6)1921; A.M. Bellamy to Smith, 24 Nov. 1921, EEF C(6)1921; 'Replies by Associations to Questionnaire dated 30 Jan. 1922', EEF M(19), App. 2; A. Herbert to Smith, 25 March 1922, EEF M(19)2. See also H.A. Clegg, *A History of British Trade Union since 1889*, Vol.II (Oxford, 1985), p.339.

34. E. Wigham, op. cit., pp.119–27; McKinlay, op. cit., pp.97–111.

35. Engineering and National Employers' Federation, *Thirty years of Industrial Conciliation* (London, 1927); p.4.

36. R. Martin, *Communism and the British Trade Unions, 1924–1933* (Oxford, 1969); A. McKinlay, op. cit., pp.143–53.

37. P. Ryan, 'Apprenticeship and Industrial Relations in British Engineering: The Early Interwar Period', unpublished paper presented to the Workshop on Child Labour and Apprenticeship, University of Essex, May 1986; Special Committee in Regard to the Supply, Selection and Training of Apprentices, 1927–29, EEF A(7)91; Subcommittee on Apprentices and Young Persons, 1933–36, EEF A(7)111; meetings, memoranda and correspondence on grading of machine operations, 1923–30, EEF M(22)1.

38. N.W.E.T.E.A., Case Papers, June 1924, Folio 23/3.

39. S. Tolliday, 'Management and Labour in Britain 1896–1939', in S. Tolliday and J. Zeitlin (eds.), *The Automobile Industry and its Workers* (Oxford, 1986), pp.37–40; W. Lewchuk, *American Technology and the British Vehicle Industry* (Cambridge, 1987), Ch.8.

40. A. McKinlay, *op. cit.*, pp.164–88; R. Croucher, *Engineers at War 1939–1945* (London, 1982), pp.24–9.

41. H. Gospel, 'Employers' Organisations: Their Growth and Function in the British System of Industrial Relations, 1918–1939', Ph.D., London, 1974, pp.180–183.

42. A. McKinlay, 'From Industrial Serf to Wage Labourer: The 1937 Apprentices' Revolt in Britain', *International Review of Social History*, Vol.XXXI (1986), pp.1–18.

EMPLOYERS' LABOUR STRATEGIES, INDUSTRIAL WELFARE, AND THE RESPONSE TO NEW UNIONISM AT BRYANT AND MAY, 1888–1930

By ROBERT FITZGERALD

I

The insight brought to the history of British industrial relations by research into labour's daily work experience is now widely recognised. What was once the narrow study of trade union organisation has been transformed into a subject incorporating questions about the work process and authority relations on the factory-floor. The debate has particularly focused on the years after 1880, when falling profits and changing technology are perceived as hardening employer attitudes towards wages, deskilling, and work-organisation. Labour's response was an increasing working class militancy which involved both the emergent New Unions of unskilled workers and the established craft societies. These changes in the direction of labour history have inevitably introduced a greater awareness of the role of employers and management, but the contribution of business historians to these issues has been comparatively muted. Too many company case studies have failed to develop themes in specific areas like industrial relations. Although employers reacted to rising working-class militancy through collective bargaining agreements and organised strike-breaking, changes in the internal management of companies have been largely overlooked.[1] Yet the New Unionism, founded at the match-makers Bryant and May and in the gas and dock industries during 1888–89, undoubtedly had an impact on companies' labour management policies.

Perspectives on the development of the business enterprise and its organisational and production requirements are of obvious benefit to understanding company-based labour management.[2] The replacement of the family firm by the large oligopolistic or monopolistic company has been a central trend in industrial history over the last hundred years. As the size of the business enterprise grew, managerial organisation and the planning of production from the raw material stage to manufacture and distribution became more important.[3] This increased in certain industries the possibilities for long-term managerial policies towards workforces beyond that of the market relationship of the wage contract.[4] The creation of internal labour markets within firms, founded on schemes of decasualisation, centrally-directed hiring and training, and welfare benefits, could be coupled with the managerial standardisation, measurement and control of work methods. The implications of work skills and changing technology may have become a central interest to labour historians, but the varied influences of markets and management structures have also to be considered if the labour strategy developed by a company like Bryant and May in the face of increasing worker militancy is to be understood.

II

The original view of New Unionism as the establishment in the late 1880s of quite unprecedented non-sectional, socialist organisations for unskilled labourers has long since been revised. Workers without specialised skills had only their collective strength with which to bargain, and, since they were often engaged in casual trades marked by underemployment, their bargaining strength was highly dependent on the trade cycle. General unions, consequently, had been formed before the late 1880s, principally during periods of high employment in 1833–35 and 1872–74. The dramatic growth in union membership in 1888–92, when it doubled to 1.5 million, was none the less unprecedented. The strike at Bryant and May in July 1888 against a system of arbitrary fines and the victimisation of trades unionists was a notable success for a largely female and casual workforce. The formation of a gasworkers' union in April 1889 led to the winning of an eight-hour day two months later, but it was the victory of the dockers the following September which had most impact on contemporaries. General union branches began to be founded throughout the country. Yet the New Unions composed just over 13 per cent of union membership in 1892, and represented less than ten per cent by 1900. The sectional, craft unions like the engineers and cotton spinners remained predominant. Moreover, the New Unions' membership generally survived only amongst its more skilled sectors such as the stevedores and lightermen. With the important exception of the gasworkers, they soon abandoned the idea of the general, all-embracing union and used their society ticket to control entry to employment. Confronted by worsening trade conditions, strike-breaking and costly legal action by employers, the New Unionism of 1892–1910 proved cautious as well as sectional. The opportunities presented by the improved economic circumstances of 1910–13 brought another wave of unionisation and strikes. There were 2.6 million trade unionists in 1910, and 4.1 million in 1913, but the figure had risen to 8.3 million or to 48 per cent of the entire workforce by 1920. Although many of the general unions could trace their origins to the temporary success of 1889, the Great War's insatiable demand for labour and the state's encouragement of collective bargaining from 1914–20 were the most significant factors in ultimately transforming their formerly precarious existence.[5]

Richard Price and others have interpreted increasing union organisation class conflict after 1880 as a result of the restructuring of work and changes in the social relations of production. The emergence of strong foreign competition forced employers to improve productivity. Workers, who had once been largely responsible for the planning and execution of production, were increasingly subjected to the division and deskilling of labour, managerial supervision, and intensive piece-rate systems. Furthermore, collective bargaining was used a means of enhancing employer control over the pace and content of work. Price, none the less, disputes Braverman's thesis that labour was ultimately subordinated by Taylorist deskilling strategies. He argues that continual workshop resistance enabled workers to maintain varying degrees of control over new techniques.[6] Price's stress upon class conflict has been criticised. While Patrick Joyce emphasises the central importance of work and the workplace, his account of the mid-nineteenth-century Lancashire cotton industry concentrates upon labour's reformism and moderation. Deference and dependence stemmed from the paternalist and interdependent social structure of the factory community which thrived around family firms. Even after 1880, argues Joyce, workers had to compromise in order to protect their own livelihood. Though the emphasis may be different, neither Price nor Joyce deny the possible coexistence of class conflict and class co-operation.[7] Moreover, they both see 1880 as marking the end of a paternalist golden age, when the atmosphere of the family firm was gradually replaced by the less personalised relations of the joint stock company and intensified class feeling.[8]

It is this demarcation of the history of industrial relations into distinctive periods which is most questionable. Evidence of bitter labour disputes in the Lancashire cotton industry of 1850–80 is too extensive to be ignored. The limits of paternalism in a trade whose profitability, employment, and wages were badly affected by trade cycles and foreign competition has also been noted.[9] Price, likewise, focuses on a narrow aspect of industrial relations from 1880–1926. The maintenance of craft skills, however, was pursued by a sectional minority of workers engaged in staple industries like engineering, cotton spinning, shipbuilding, and construction. The level of deskilling in these industries is also exaggerated. They remained unrationalised and highly reliant upon flexible work-skills due to the need to respond quickly to changing and varied markets. Government support for employer – employee negotiations during the Great War and better union organisation proved more important for the majority of unskilled workers than workshop resistance, simply because they depended solely on their collective strength, and had no specific skills to protect. The course of labour relations and the levels of class conflict in different markets, industries, and companies was diverse, and varied from decade to decade.[10]

Joyce's emphasis upon the culture of the mid-nineteenth-century factory tends to overlook paternalism's economic rationale. Price follows this theme, and, in turn, sees New Unionism as a symptom of the demise of a traditional paternal authority.[11] The managerial reasons underlying paternalism were just as valid after 1880 as before. Employers needed to develop the means of maintaining the supply and quality of labour.[12] They had to try and resolve the dilemma that, although businesses and production ultimately depended on a level of co-operation, the employment relationship produced an inherent conflict over profits and wages. Employers benefited from seeking to prevent strikes, work disaffection, and resistance to managerial direction, although the potential for class conflict, given the nature of the employment relationship, was always present. The greater stability and profitability of markets, more sophisticated managerial structures, larger company size, and the need to retain firm-specific skills all encouraged labour management policies beyond those of the wage contract. Internal labour markets – based on the central direction of hiring and training, the managerial standardisation and planning of work methods, or welfare schemes – were particularly necessary in monopolies like the railways and in the oligopolistic corporations which came to dominate the twentieth-century economy. Changes in company organisation made the paternalism of the small family firm inadequate, but encouraged the development of systemised welfare schemes.[13]

Just as deskilling strategies were limited in the staple industries after 1880, the intense competition they faced, their small firm size, and weak managerial structures discouraged the formation of extensive internal labour markets. Although Taylor's Scientific Management had little influence on British management, the Bedaux company established during the inter-war years a refined form of Taylorism. It was adopted by some companies largely in 'new' industries like chemicals and food processing, where little deskilling was experienced due to the low level of skills traditionally demanded. Bedaux's methods sought to standardise work methods through the detailed managerial monitoring of each worker, and it encouraged effort through the payment of bonuses. Although management became directly involved in the organisation of work methods, Littler still asserts that the Bedaux system did not promote internal labour markets. While companies may have adopted the system in order to speed up work, it did also represent a managerial commitment to the planning of production and manpower budgetting. Like Price and Joyce, Littler looks for evidence of paternalism as an expression of class reciprocity at a time when it had become in the main inappropriate, and he underestimates the expanding role of internal markets and industrial welfare as tools of labour management.[14] Evidence from the United States suggests that after 1880 companies became increasingly interested in both the standardisation and planning of work methods and in systemised company provision, and it is an approach which might profitably be applied to Britain.[15]

Employers responded to New Unionism and growing working class unrest by adopting a number of labour strategies, including internal management methods and industrial welfare. They were used by companies in the three industries of matchmaking, gas, and port transport where New Unionism had its origins in 1888–89. The different influences of markets and levels of managerial organisation have a bearing on the nature of labour management in each of these cases. These differences

explain why the metropolitan gas industry was able to develop permanent and effective managerial policies in response to New Unionism,
whereas the measures taken by the docks companies proved temporary.
The growth of unions at Bryant and May's factories followed the national
pattern of rapid expansion after1888 and, more substantially, between
1910–20. As a consequence, the company's labour policies underwent
significant developments during these two periods, but changes just after
the turn of the century in industrial structure, managerial organisation
and technology were as critical in resolving the scale and exact nature
of the responses as the increasing strength of organised labour itself.
The years 1910–20 were the most significant in determining industrial
relations at Bryant and May. The company, moreover, is a prime case
of how (contrary to the impression given by Price and Joyce) the value
of welfare schemes increased after 1880. It was a firm which had relied
to some extent on domestic outwork, and employed a mainly casual,
female labour force. It demonstrated little interest in its workers beyond
the payment of low wages, and profitability and employment in the firm
was continually threatened by intense competition. Labour management
at Bryant and May in the 1880s, therefore, was minimalist, but it was to
develop into a prominent welfarist employer.

III

The poverty, insecurity, and underemployment of casual labour was
epitomised by dock work. The flow of cargoes was affected by the
seasonality of trade and weather conditions, and a ready pool of labour
suited employers. The disadvantages of casualism, however, were also
perceived. Dockers, who owed no loyalty to a company, were seen as ill-
disciplined and unreliable. From the early nineteenth century, therefore,
London employers had attempted to establish a core of permanent workers, but all these attempts were undermined by the advantages which
the flexibility of the casual system offered to dock companies. The 1889
strike was directed at curbing the worst aspects of casualism. The Dock,
Wharf, Riverside and General Labourers' Union obtained an agreement
guaranteeing at least four hours' employment on each job, the abolition
of sub-contracting, a fairer division of piece-work bonuses, and a minimum of 6d. an hour. Support for the strike was centred at the London
and India Docks Co., the port's largest employer, where the continuation of minor disputes was viewed as more damaging than the original
strike. London dock labour had seemingly become unmanageable, and
a sharp fall in productivity was blamed on the recently-imposed closed
shop. As a result, the employers ended union control over the hiring
of workers in November 1890, and, faced with dissatisfaction over
its management of the Victoria and Albert and Tilbury docks, their
operation was handed over to the shipowners. Elsewhere, the company
in December 1890 established a system of permanent men as a means of
combatting the unions, increasing discipline, and encouraging effort and

company loyalty. Permanent workers enjoyed job security, sick pay of ten shillings a week through membership of a compulsory friendly society, pay for statutory holidays and three days' annual leave, and, after 15 years' service, a non-contributory pension of between 6 and 12 shillings. Registered or 'A' workers were hired on a weekly basis, obtained holiday benefit, and could be promoted to the permanent staff with half of their previous service counting towards a pension. Preference or 'B' workers were given tickets numbered according to seniority, which provided them with the first call on employment after the Registered workers but before the casuals. By offers of job security and welfare benefits, the company reasserted control over its workforce, and the dockers' union labelled the permanent workers 'white slaves'. The company employed 1750 of them in 1891 – in addition to some 3,000 Registered and Preferred men and 1500 casuals – but their numbers continued to decline. Throughout London in 1904, permanent men constituted about two per cent of the dock labour force. The Port of London Authority, which took over the running of the docks in 1909, retained permanent men. They joined strikes in 1911 and 1912, and the Authority replaced them with blacklegs. 3,000 permanent workers were officially appointed in October 1914, but welfare benefits were removed. Although, therefore, support for de-casualisation had grown in the years after 1889, dock employers in general continued to view permanent men as less productive. This was partly because they were seen as complacent and cushioned by job security, and partly because they had always to be employed even when temporary specialised labour was more appropriate.[16]

Company welfare proved more successful in the metropolitan gas industry. Production was capital-intensive, and firm and plant size grew dramatically in the 1870s until the Gas Light and Coke and South Metropolitan Gas companies dominated London's output. Employers, however, continued to rely on the manual efforts of a core workforce of stokers, whose workloads were speeded up to meet rising demand. When the National Union of Gasworkers and General Labourers in July 1889 successfully demanded an eight-hour day and a reduction in the pace of work, they were voicing grievances held for nearly a quarter of a century. The SMGC sought to win back the loyalty of its workforce through profit-sharing, and a strike, called on the issue of the scheme and lasting from December 1889 to February 1890, was defeated by the employment of non-union blackleg labour. The GLCC, unlike the South Metropolitan, never banned the gasworkers' union, but both companies from the 1890s adopted policies of systematic welfare provision. Profitsharing, pensions, sick pay, accident benefits, and recreational facilities were the means used to instil the loyalty the companies required from key workers engaged in an essential supply industry. The written rules, guaranteed benefits, self-management, and contributory nature of the industry's schemes replaced notions of *ex gratia* paternalism. They were not 'holding operations', as Price states, but an effective approach to ensuring that no major dispute occurred after 1889. Welfare supported the gradual de-casualisation of the industry, whose employment-levels were influenced by the seasonal demand for light. Greater mechanisation after 1889 reduced the number of men engaged in the retort-house to between a sixth and a quarter of previous numbers. Together with an expanding non-seasonal demand for cooking and industrial purposes, it reduced the variation in the total employed from summer to winter from 53.4 per cent in 1885 to 20.4 per cent in 1906. More permanent workers, moreover, were employed in outdoor departments as fitters or meter readers to serve a larger, more working-class clientele. The job security of an internal labour market and industrial welfare were central to the gas industry's labour strategy after 1889.[17]

IV

Bryant and May was founded in 1839 as a firm of general merchants by the Quakers William Bryant and Francis May. In 1855, the company obtained the British patent over the safety match, and, six years later, began its manufacture at the Fairfield Works in London's East End. The new factory was well-planned and ventilated, and received a favourable report from the 1862 Royal Commission on the Employment of Children in Industry. It was, however, William Bryant's son, Wilberforce, who gave the lead to his three brothers and fellow directors by securing the company's early dominance of British matchmaking. During the 1860s, the industry was almost entirely a manual process. From 1874, Bryant extended the works in order to install machinery. His aim was to meet the quantity and quality demanded by the growing market for safety matches. He also needed to combat low-priced imports from the Continent, which by the 1870s accounted for 20 per cent of sales. Within a few years, the Fairfield factory was re-equipped with 300 of the latest automatic machines capable of a daily output of nearly 1.75m boxes of safety matches. Matchmaking emerged as a highly capital-intensive industry. Bryant was, moreover, instrumental in introducing other successful products like wax vestas, and he made the firm aware of the importance of advertising and brand loyalty. In 1884, the firm became a limited company with £400,000 in capital, and it was soon using its resources to buy out British competitors. Wilberforce Bryant became its first chairman, and remained in that post till 1906.[18]

The machinery installed after 1874 dealt mainly with the fitting of match splints into frames, prior to their being dipped into the various chemicals with which matches were impregnated or covered.[19] Wood, when it arrived at the factory, was mechanically slit into splints. These were loaded into a hopper, which fed them into large revolving drums composed of flexible metal bands and dotted with holes through which the splints fell and were held in place. A coiling machine was able at that point to enclose the drums in webbing to form frames of 15 inches in diameter. These frames were dipped in paraffin to ensure the matches would burn, and in ammonium sulphate to prevent them smouldering when extinguished. After being heat-dried, the splints were dipped at both ends in chlorate of potash and sulphur, which ignited when rubbed against the amorphous phosphorus on the side of matchboxes. After being heat-dried once more, the frames went to the decoiling machines. The splints were then placed in bunches on a hand-operated cutting machine by female workers, who, with great accuracy, severed each splint into two matches. These were subsequently placed on a machine which packed them into boxes, and finally the covers were slid on.

The division of labour was strictly patriarchial.[20] Male foremen were in charge of the factory-floor, and exercised the authority to hire and fire. The work of the dippers was equally a preserve for men. They were considered the 'labour aristocrats' of the industry, and were assisted by apprentices. The vast majority of employees, however, were women, and were basically divided into fillers (of the splints into the coiled frames), cutters-down, and packers. Output was measured, and each worker was paid by the piece. Not every female operative was employed at the factory, and those engaged in matchbox-making and the printing of labels were domestic out-workers. One commentator in 1876 estimated that some 5,000 persons directly or indirectly laboured for Bryant and May, although employment was highly seasonal. The matchgirls, many of whom were Irish, lived largely in Bow and Whitechapel, and were seen as a tightly-knit and distinctive group. Engaged on casual piece-work, they demonstrated little company loyalty, and were criticised for their chronic absenteeism, unreliability, and lack of discipline. Like so many in the great concentration of sweated trades situated in the East End, their poverty was perceived as giving rise to a culture which challenged accepted 'Victorian' values. Bryant and May attempted to control this workforce by a regime of strict but arbitrary discipline. Wilberforce Bryant in 1888 recognised that piece-work made the company's workers 'rather independent' in their attitude to attendance at the factory. Fines and charges for materials were seen as a legitimate means of instilling discipline and thrifty work practices, and as inevitable given the numbers and type of workers Bryant and May employed. The directors, on the other hand, were criticised for their lack of involvement at the factory-floor and for their total reliance on the discretion of foremen.[21]

A little-known strike at the firm in 1885 failed, but publicity and public opinion won the matchgirls' famous victory three years' later. Their grievances were published by the Fabian Annie Besant in *The Link* of June 1888. She reported on bullying foremen, low wages, and long, irregular hours. Fines were imposed for untidiness, talking, damages to the product or to the machinery, and for breaks in production even when they resulted from minor personal injury. Latecomers were shut out for the morning with the consequent loss of half a day's wages. There were no separate washing or lunch facilities despite the unhealthy atmosphere in the factory. Concern was also expressed at the unchecked incidence of 'phossy-jaw', a form of necrosis around the mouth and gums caused by contact with phosphorus. Moreover, resentment had solidified around accusations that one shilling had been compulsorily deducted from wages by Theodore Bryant (Wilberforce's brother) in order to erect a statue to Gladstone. The unpaid half-holiday held for its unveiling intensified feelings. Bryant and May responded by sacking the three workers known to have talked to Besant, who immediately appealed for funds and a commercial boycott of the firm. When the employers in July attempted to obtain the girls' signatures to a declaration countering *The Link*'s allegations, all 1,400 of them walked out. Besant herself did not believe that sweating could be cured by unionisation, due to the problems of organising casual and underemployed workers. She nevertheless agreed to lead the spontaneous strike. Bryant and May on the 16th July conceded the matchgirls' demands. All fines and deductions for work materials were removed – in part because the Factory Inspectorate concluded they breached the Truck Acts – and large cuts were restored. The 'pennies' were also returned. These were a payment taken by the firm from the box-fillers to pay for assistant carriers, who enabled the achievement of greater levels of piece-work. The money had continued to be deducted even though Bryant and May had ceased to employ the assistants. In addition, no victimisation and union recognition were agreed, and all grievances were to be put to management before strike action took place. The Union of Women Matchmakers had its official inaugural meeting on 27 July 1888, and could claim 666 members by October. After the strike, both Bryant and May and Besant found they could amicably resolve disputes and stoppages. Union membership, however, began to fall by the end of the year.[22]

Bryant and May also promised in the strike agreement to consider providing a room for meal-times. A union club was established after the strike, but soon closed. A rival organisation, Clifden House, was founded by Bryant and May in 1889. It offered workers cheap meals and a place to relax under the charge of a lady superintendent. The managing director George Bartholomew was directly responsible for the company's increasing support for the club.[23] While fines and deductions were a common means amongst the casual trades for imposing discipline,[24] the attention of the factory inspectorate and the strike agreement had forced Bryant and May to seek other methods. The lady superintendent, a Miss Nash, was appointed to use the club's societies, classes and entertainments to instill self-improvement, temperance, and better behaviour. Moreover, her role in making grievances known to the company headed off disputes and bypassed the union. Excursions and sporting clubs also improved relations at the company.[25] By 1895, Bryant and May engaged 1,000 women and 300 men and boys at the Fairfield works, and another 700 workers at its Bow Common and tin-box factories. For Bartholomew, the chief difficulty with matchgirls was countering their 'don't care' attitude to time-keeping and regular attendance. The club's beneficial effect on work discipline was recognised, and this influence was extended by the superintendent's visits to the girls' homes. She promoted stability and Christian ideals, and thrift was encouraged with the establishment of a Savings Club. Mothers' meetings and Christmas treats provided for the matchgirls' families, and bolstered 'domestic values'. Labour relations were described as 'cordial'.[26]

Despite changes in Bryant and May's managerial attitudes since 1888, circumstances did not yet necessitate a coherent welfarist strategy. It was the technological changes introduced from the 1890s onwards which altered fundamentally the structure and management of the industry.[27] The United State's Diamond Match Corporation produced the first continuous-process matchmaking machine, and, in 1895, began the construction of the world's largest match factory in Liverpool.[28] Wood was sliced into blocks which could be revolved for the peeling of strips of veneer the thickness of a match. These strips then travelled through a series of machines which cut them into matchsticks. After being boiled in huge tanks of ammonium phosphate to facilitate the extinguishing of the final product, the sticks were dried and polished by being blown through large wind tunnels. They were eventually deposited in hoppers at the top of the factory, from where they fell on to screens which bounced and aligned the sticks. They were then punched mechanically into drums studded with holes so that they could easily be dipped in paraffin wax and then into the igniting composition. After being dried by fans, the matches were punched out of the drums into a flowing stream of steel slots the size of matchboxes. Their contents were loaded into boxes, over which their covers were slipped. The matchboxes were also made by the use of machines and wind tunnels.[29] The introduction of automatic machinery at every process-stage coupled with pneumatic transfer dramatically increased through-put. Diamond thereby greatly undercut the price of Bryant and May's matches.

Although the Americans' competitive position was stronger, the regional brand loyalties Bryant and May enjoyed throughout Britain still made an inter-company arrangement valuable. Diamond, furthermore, was intent on arriving at world-wide agreements with major producers as a means of introducing a degree of market stability. The threat of continental low-wage competition continued even after the 1890s. Obtaining the patents to the continuous process had become so vital to Bryant and May's survival that, by 1901, it accepted the mutual benefits of amalgamation. On 28 June, Bryant and May paid £480,000 to buy out the British Diamond Co. but, in return, had to give Diamond 54.4 per cent of the newly-enlarged Bryant and May's shares. Diamond agreed not to sell in the British Empire and Commonwealth excepting in the West Indies, and Bryant and May guaranteed not to manufacture in North America and to limit exports there to levels achieved in 1900. Within a year, Bryant and May's profits had doubled. The new machinery was installed at Fairfield in 1904, but, in 1909, the works was transferred to a new building at Bow. When completed in 1911, it made 10,000 million matches and 100,000 miles of wax vestas or tapers per annum. A secure home market was intended as a base for expansion overseas

in order to overcome tariff barriers. By 1905, Bryant and May had a
virtual monopoly in Australia, New Zealand, and South Africa. The
company proved to be so successful and expansionary that by 1914 it
had bought back all the shares which had passed to Diamond in 1901,
and became once more a fully independent company. In 1921, it made
an agreement with Diamond to secure the Canadian market, and other
subsidiaries were formed throughout the world in the 1920s. Foreign
imports continued, however, to undermine sales, and, in 1927, Bryant
and May united with the Swedish Match Company to form the British
Match Corporation. It was a holding company, capitalised at £6m, 70 per
cent of which belonged to Bryant and May.[30]

Fears about the continuous process brought about an unsuccessful
strike at the Fairfield Works in 1902. This failure on the part of
the Matchmakers' Union was a consequence of the long-term fall in
its membership, and confirmed the effectiveness of the company's
calculated fostering of harmonious industrial relations. The union was
wound up the following year.[31] Bryant and May, in fact, introduced the
new technology with little difficulty, and great attention continued to be
paid to factory conditions in the early 1900s. The new Fairfield Works
at Bow and the Diamond Works at Liverpool were well ventilated and
lighted, and had wash-rooms, launderies, cloakrooms, and canteens.
Doctors' surgeries, dental treatment, and first aid were also available.
The Diamond Works opened a girls' club in 1910, and the Fairfield institute persisted with the promotion of 'improving' activities.[32] But labour
relations were altered by the general resurgence of unionism after 1911.
By 1912, most Bryant and May workers had joined the National Union of
Gas Workers and General Labourers.[33] In January 1912, 600 matchgirls
at Bow walked out in support of 24 members of the Amalgamated
Society of Engineers who refused to work excessive overtime and sought
better pay for their highly specialised skills. In June, Bryant and May
was surprised when all of Fairfield's 1,200 workers unofficially struck
in protest at the dismissal of an engineer for unsatisfactory work. The
Gasworkers and General Union, however, preferred to avoid a dispute
and negotiated an early return to work. It had become clear, none the
less, that the continuous process enabled a single department to close
down the whole factory.[34] While work conditions at Bryant and May
were those of a model employer, the company had not yet developed the
managerial techniques required by its new technology, size, and market
share. Large-scale capital investment had ended all domestic outwork
and concentrated production in the factory. The continuous process
had increased the company's reliance on the co-operation of labour at
each production stage. By having to plan output over a large enterprise
for an increasingly oligopolistic market, Bryant and May had the need
and the resources to secure required levels of manpower, skills, and
worker co-operation. But the company had not by 1914 perceived the
usefulness of encouraging an internal labour market through a system of
organised benefits like sick pay or pensions. It did in that year, however,

recognise the consequences of expansion for the role of management, and established a staff pension fund. It received equal contributions from employee and company, and was intended to build up a stable and loyal managerial workforce.[35]

George Paton, Bryant and May's chairman since 1911, acknowledged that manpower shortages and the unions' increased bargaining power necessitated a positive response. His post-war welfare strategy, which emerged as a consequence of the conflict, was nonetheless a conscious recognition of the impact changes in technology and changes in the company's size and structure had had on labour policies. The new-found strength of the unions brought industry-wide collective bargaining, and made a company-based, systematic welfare policy more urgent.[36] Paton became in July 1918 the first chairman of the Matchmaking Joint Industrial Council which, in 1919, introduced a 47-hour week and paid annual holidays.[37] Local works councils complemented the National Council. They provided a forum for management–worker discussion on all labour and welfare matters. At Bryant and May, they put a particular emphasis on explaning company regulations, works discipline, time-keeping, and the quality of production. By 1919, workers were appearing before the Fairfield Works Committee to explain bad timekeeping, and, according to the number of penalty marks they had acquired, were threatened with the sack or dismissed. The names of girls reported for the poor quality of their work were placed on a noticeboard. Works Committees also assumed responsibility for safety and suggestions schemes. Statistics on absenteeism and sickness were carefully monitored.[38] Good time-keeping was portrayed as mutually beneficial to the company and to workers after the founding of a co-partnership scheme in 1919. 200,000 shares were created to pay dividends to the Brymay Partnership Trust Limited. Workers and staff could take their bonus in cash or in shares, and those who accrued 50 partnership shares could exercise the right of any ordinary shareholder. Bryant and May argued that co-partnership increased labour's interest in the prosperity of the company, and provided workers with greater financial security. £24,000 was distributed in 1920, and £42,000 in 1921. The worth of bonuses rose from 6.38 per cent of wages to 11.5 per cent in 1927, and, by 1928, there were 91,444 £1 partnership shares. These represented just over two per cent of the company's capital. Though the Trust was nominally run by a committee of directors and elected workers, it was totally controlled by Paton and C.E. Bartholomew.[39] In 1919, the company also founded a Non-Contributory Life Insurance scheme. It offered, at the discretion of the company, £10 per year of service to the dependants of deceased employees, so long as the sum did not exceed £200. Life assurance met the immediate plight of families who had lost their breadwinner, which was seen as a common fear haunting workers and thereby damaging industrial relations.[40]

Labour representatives on the earliest Works Committees called for the founding of sick pay and pension schemes, but Bryant and May hesitated over the cost involved.[41] Under the copartnership scheme, however, the bonuses of those the company had employed less than a year or whose work was designated unsatisfactory or irregular were paid to the Bryant and May Benefit Fund. Participation in the copartnership scheme, like payment for holidays, depended upon good conduct and time-keeping. The fund provided medical assistance, sick pay, superannuation allowances, pensions, and also marriage dowries. The last were intended as compensation for the large number of young women who left before being in a position to obtain pension benefits. In 1921, the Fund received £5,000, and, in 1922, £13,000. Like the Trust, the Fund was controlled by Paton and Bartholomew. Its investments amounted to over £40,000 in 1929.[42] The *Brymay Magazine* began publication in October of that year as a means of communicating with workers, building up a corporate identity, and promoting welfare benefits. It reported on sports, recreational, and educational clubs, canteens, excursions, holiday funds, and medical and dental facilities at each works, and on the company-wide Bryant and May Athletic Association and the Savings Bank.[43] Different factories within the group continued to organise their own welfare activities. The Bryant and May Employees' Hospital and Benevolent Fund was founded at Fairfield in 1918.[44] An inaccurately-named Tontine Society, offering sick pay, convalescent treatment, and funeral benefits in return for contributions, had existed since 1900 at the Diamond Works, and during the 1920s similar organisations were founded throughout Bryant and May. They were slate clubs which at Christmas equitably divided their assets between members. Payments from a Tontine Society did not, however, exclude anyone from obtaining the Benefit Fund's assistance.[45] A Supplementary Voluntary Employee Benefit Scheme was founded in 1921 by the Joint Industrial Council to provide additional benefits under the Unemployment Insurance Act 1920. Companies paid a sum equal to one per cent of their wages bill until a total of five per cent was reached, and further payments were used to maintain this figure. Companies, however, retained the right to alter or discontinue contributions. Union membership was a condition of participating in the scheme, and trades unions collected two pence weekly for part of the benefits received. The scheme offered 50 per cent of average wages, plus, for male employees, ten per cent for a dependent wife, and five per cent for each dependent child under 16, with a maximum payment of 75 per cent of earnings. From this sum, state benefits and the six shillings received from the union were deducted. The periods of assistance, ranging from three to 43 weeks, were determined by an individual's length of service. Works committees were charged with guarding against malingerers. The scheme aimed to remove workers' anxieties about the effects of cyclical and seasonal fluctuations. It also combined class co-operation with protecting the position of the union.[46]

Industrial welfare at Bryant and May's welfare schemes recognised the human dimension in industry, and was 'not luxury, nor a philanthropy, but has a definite integral place in factory organisation'. Bryant and May acknowledged that the firm's success depended on the cooperation of workers. Industry, it was argued, could not merely pursue profit, but had to be conducted for the benefit of all who participated in it. Paton stressed the loyalty of Bryant and May's workforce, and he believed that welfare explained the fact that not one employee struck during the General Strike of 1926. For Paton, copartnership deterred strikes by making labour feel it owned its place of work and by providing a fair wage. Healthy and contented workers secured greater effort and efficiency. Teamwork was essential if cheap imports from the Continent were to be combatted. Moreover, Paton argued, copartnership 'encourages long service and the minimum number of changes in personnel, which means that a better standard of work is maintained; for obviously new hands mean temporary losses while they learn their work'.[47] The system, therefore, encouraged an internal labour market in work experience and labour skills. The replacement of hiring by foremen by the more systematic methods of the 1920s reflected the institutionalising of seniority and the greater prospects for long-term employment. New recruits were engaged according a central waiting list, and underwent a medical examination. The Unemployment Insurance scheme, like short-time, was used as a means of maintaining a labour force in times of economic depression. While labour turnover had stood at 69 per cent before the important post-war schemes were introduced, the figure for 1929 was quoted as being in practical terms non-existent. A more stable workforce was seen as an important factor in Bryant and May's ability to manufacture a quality product.[48] The company's policy of rationalisation and stream-lining was far-sighted. Its size protected its market, and enabled it explicitly to offer and promote security for its staff, workers, shareholders. Effective labour management was part of a successful commercial organisation.[49]

V

Industrial welfare and the encouragement of a cooperative workforce increased rather than declined in importance after 1880, due to the managerial, organisational, and market requirements of the twentieth-century firm. Moreover, growing unionisation and class conflict in gas and matchmaking – far from undermining the rationale of company provision – spurred the development of a welfare strategy. After 1888–89, gas employers systemised their provident schemes, while Bryant and May improved work conditions as a means of countering the influence of the union. The match company's policy was a response to the difficulties of employing in the East End's casual labour market. It was not until the changes in technology, work organisation, and company size that Bryant and May required a welfare policy like that of gas employers. This was introduced, nevertheless, partly as the result of the final, successful unionisation of its workforce during the Great War. The docks companies, however, did not undergo Bryant and May's changes in size and managerial organisation, and failed to develop internal labour markets or viable welfare strategies. Furthermore, the introduction of automatic, continuous machinery did not lead to deliberate deskilling and greater casualisation, but to an increased reliance on labour's co-operation and firm-specific skills. The type of industrial welfare adopted at Bryant and May was not as some commentators have implied, merely an 'anachronistic' expression of mutual goodwill, but a practical and effective means of resolving the conflicting interests of employers and workers. A combination of appalling conditions in the 1880s and the labour management requirements of later years challenges the idea of industrial welfare as the product of Quaker or Christian philanthropy on the part of employers. Quakerism did not provide employers with a single, coherent business philosophy, but instead could only lay claim to a number of very different individuals who happened to be industrialists. The lessons to be drawn from religious conviction produced both the socially conscious Rowntrees and Cadburys and the avaricious and harsh Bryant brothers. Devoutness was no guarantee of philanthropy.[50] Indeed, it was the professional managers like Bartholomew and Paton, who increasingly took over the running of the firm, that were responsible for making Bryant and May a welfarist employer. In contrast to Wilberforce Bryant, who acknowledged only his duty to shareholders,[51] Paton argued that the rights to profits had to be balanced alongside the interests of workers. Although Bryant and May remained an avowedly Christian firm, religious motives were notably absent in the explicit reasons given for its most important advances in welfare during the inter-war years. Other factors were always more determinate. Company provision was extended to cope with the changes in labour requirements brought about by alterations in the firm's size, structure, market, and technology, and in trade unionist strength. Bryant and May found solutions to the developing realities of commercial and labour management.

Business History Unit,
London School of Economics

NOTES

My thanks are due to Bryant and May Ltd. and the Hackney Archives Department, and to Mary Achillea, Stephen Gruneberg, Dr Howard Gospel, Professor Leslie Hannah, Greg Marchildon and Dr John Turner for their comments on the first draft of this article.

  1. See, however, J. Melling, 'Industrial Strife and Business Welfare Philosophy: The Case of the South Metropolitan Gas Company from the 1880s to the War,' *Business History,* Vol.XXI, No.2 (1979), pp.163–79.
  2. H.F, Gospel and C.R. Littler (eds.), *Managerial Strategies and Industrial Relations,* (London, 1983).

3. L. Hannah, *The Rise of the Corporate Economy* (London, 1976).
4. Fitzgerald, *British Labour Management and Industrial Welfare, 1846–1939* (London, 1988).
5. J. Lovell, *British Trade Unions, 1875–1933* (1977); H.A. Clegg *et. al., A History of British Trade Unions Since 1889*, Vols. I and II (Oxford, 1964, 1985); W.J. Mommsen and H.-G. Husung (eds.), *The Development of Trade Unionism in Great Britain and Germany, 1880–1914* (London, 1985).
6. R. Price, *Masters, Unions and Men* (Cambridge, 1980); 'The Labour Process and Labour History', *Social History*, Vol.VIII, No.1 (1983), pp.57–75; 'The New Unionism and the Labour Process' in Mommsen and Husung, op. cit., pp.133–7; *Labour in British Society* (London, 1986), pp.1–14. See also K. Burgess, *The Origins of British Industrial Relations* (London, 1975); and H. Braverman, *Labor and Monopoly Capital* (New York, 1974).
7. P. Joyce, *Work, Society and Politics* (London, 1980); 'Labour, Capital and Compromise: A Response to Richard Price', *Social History*, Vol.9, No.1 (1984), pp.67–76; R. Price, 'Conflict and Co-operation: A Reply to Patrick Joyce, *Social History*, Vol.9, No.2 (1984) pp.217–24; P. Joyce, 'Languages of Reciprocity and Conflict: A Further Response to Richard Price', *Social History*, Vol.9, No.2 (1984), pp.225–31.
8. Price, *Labour in British Society*, pp.71–93; Joyce, *Work, Society, and Politics*, pp.331–44.
9. H.I. Dutton and J.E. King 'The Limits of Paternalism: The Cotton Tyrants of North Lancashire, 1836–54', *Social History*, Vol.7, No.1 (1982), pp.59–74; and 'Ten Per Cent and No Surrender': The Preston Strike, 1853–54 (1981); N. Kirk, *The Growth of Working Class Reformism in Mid-Victorian England* (London, 1985), pp.1–31, 241–309.
10. Mommsen and Husung, op. cit., pp.150–56, 325–34; J. Zeitlin 'The Labour Strategies of British Engineering Employers, 1890–1922' in Gospel and Littler, op. cit., pp.25–54.
11. Price, *Labour in British Society*, pp.111–27.
12. M.Huberman, 'Invisible Handshakes in Lancashire: Cotton Spinning in the First Half of the Nineteenth Century', *Journal of Economic History*, Vol.46 (1986), pp.987–98; 'The Economic Origins of Paternalism': Lancashire Cotton Spinning in the First Half of the Nineteenth Century', *Social History*, Vol.12, No.2 (1987), pp.177–92.
13. See Fitzgerald, op. cit., *passim*.
14. C.R. Littler, *The Development of the Labour Process in Capitalist Societies* (London, 1982), pp.1–5, 19, 26, 36–63, 90–97, 108–16, 133–42, 194.
15. See D. Nelson, *Managers and Workers* (Wisconsin, 1972); D. Nelson and S. Campbell 'Taylorism Versus Welfare Work in American Industry: H. L. Gantt and the Bancrofts', *Business History Review*, Vol.46 (1972), pp.1–16. On Britain, for example, a re-examination of the importance attached in the 1920s to the standardisation of work-methods at the well-known welfarist firm of Rowntrees would prove instructive.
16. Royal Commission on Labour, PP 1892 (C.6708–V), XXXV 1, QQ.4583, 4593–4, 4608–20, 4635, 4667, 4672, 4714–32, 4873–9; Select Committee on Shop Clubs, PP 1899 (C.9203), XXXIII 871, pp.vii and 15, QQ.143–8, 198; J.G. Broodbank, *History of the Port of London*, Vols.I and II (1921), pp.244, 256–9, 317, 425–57; G.Phillips and N. Whiteside, *Casual Labour: The Unemployment Question in the Port Transport Industry, 1880–1970* (Oxford, 1985), pp.1–29, 50–70, 146–75, 208–34, 283–4.
17. Melling, op. cit.; E. Hobsbawn, 'British Gas-workers 1873–1914', in *Labouring Men* (London, 1986), pp.158–78; Fitzgerald, op. cit., pp.53–76; F. Popplewell, 'The Gas Industry', in S. Webb and A. Freeman, *Seasonal Trades* (London, 1912), pp.148–209. Written accounts of the Metropolitan gas industry in 1889–90 differ greatly over crucial dates. The dates quoted throughout this article are taken from *Journal of Gas Lighting*, 28 April 1889, p.778; 9 July 1889, pp.65, 130; 17 Dec. 1889, p.1145; 11 Feb. 1890, p.249. On Price, see *Labour in British Society*, pp.114–19. On p.118, Price states that the South Metropolitan's profit-sharing scheme lasted until the 1920s, when, in fact, it survived until nationalisation in 1948.
18. D.J. Jeremy, *Dictionary of Business Biography* (London, 1984), Vol.I, pp.488–92; Hackney Archives Department, D/B/BRY/1/2/622, W. Lucas 'Bryant and May:

History' (typescript, 1958), pp.31–2, 46–7, 52, 58, 60; P.H. Emden, *Quakers in Commerce* (London, 1940), p.167; W. Lucas, *Match Making* (1956), p.6, and *Making Matches, 1861–1961* (London, 1961), pp.13, 17, 20.

19. D/B/BRY/1/2/622, Lucas, typescript, pp.47, 60.
20. See Joyce, *Work, Society, and Politics*, p.181.
21. Lucas, *Making Matches*, pp.2, 11; D/B/BRY/1/2/628, draft article by for *Brymay Magazine*; W. Glenny Crory, *East London Industries* (London, 1876), pp.42–50; D/B/BRY/1/2/622, Lucas, typescript, pp.62–4; *Times*, 12 July 1888. p.12; *Morning Advertiser,* 1 Aug. 1888,pp.5–6. See also H. Manchester, *Fifty Years of Match Making* (New York, 1928).pp.8–14. The presence of forewomen is recorded in *The Treasury*, June 1915, pp.244–9. On East London Labour conditions in the later nineteenth century, see G.S. Jones, *Outcast London* (Oxford, 1971).
22. A.H. Nethercot, *The First Five Lives of Annie Besant* (London, 1961), pp.270–75; S. Boston, *Women Workers and the Trade Union Movement* (London, 1980), pp.48–51; A. Besant, *An Autobiography* (1938), pp.335–7. See also *The Link*, 23 June 1888, pp.1–2; 30 June 1888, p.3; 7 July 1888, p.3; 14 July 1888, pp.1–4; 21 July 1888, p.3; 28 July 1888, p.3–4; 4 Aug. 1888, p.3; 11 Aug. 1988, p.4; 17 Aug. 1888, p.4. The causes of the strike were, not surprisingly, disputed. *The Link*'s description of the plight of the match girls was undoubtedly committed. The depth of the workers' feelings about their grievances, however, and their solidarity during the strike cannot be doubted. It is hard to accept Wilberforce Bryant's contention that they were apparently 'perfectly content' before the arrival of agitators. Although Bryant denied the compulsory deductions for Gladstone's statue, the imposition of fines, charges for materials, lack of facilities, and at least some of the wage reductions were admitted and conceded in the strike settlement. See T.A.B. Corley 'How Quakers Coped with Business Success: Quaker Industrialists, 1860–1914' in D.J. Jeremy (ed.), *Business and Religion in Britain* (London, 1988), pp.179,187; *The Times*, 12 July 1888. p.12 and 14 July 1888, p.9; *Morning Advertiser*, 1 Aug.1888, pp.5–6.
23. D/B/BRY/1/2/622, Lucas, typescript, pp.70–71, 92; D/B/BRY/1/2/628, *Girls' Own Paper*, 7 Dec. 1895, pp.147–9.
24. E. Cadbury *et al., Women's Work and Wages* (1907), pp.200–201, 265–73.
25. D/B/BRY/1/2/539, 1890, and 4 July 1891.
26. D/B/BRY/1/2/628, *Girls' Own Paper*, 7 Dec. 1895, pp.147–9; D/B/BRY/1/ 2/540, Match Girls Club, 27 and 29 Dec. 1897; 6, 13, 19 Jan. 1898; April 1898; May, 1898; 25 June 1898; 1 Aug. 1898; 10 Nov. 1898; 26 and 28 Dec. 1898.
27. Price argues that gas stokers and their union absorbed socialism due to the undermining of paternalist authority through conflict over changes in technology and work organisation. On the other hand, he contends, a partial reason why the match-girls failed to absorb a socialist doctrine which could sustain union membership was that social relations in match-making remained unaltered. See *Labour in British Society*, p.147. In fact, the changes in match-making technology proved critical to the industry's history.
28. A.D. Chandler, *The Visible Hand* (Cambridge, MA, 1977), pp.250, 292–3, 350, 414.
29. W.H. Beable, *Romance of Great Businesses* (London, 1926), pp.201–5; Lucas, *Match Making*, pp.7, 14, 18–31, 39.
30. D/B/BRY/1/2/622, Lucas, typescript, pp.54–61, 77–97, 102–12, 117; Lucas, *Making Matches*, pp.5–6, 11, 17, 20–25; D/B/BRY/1/2/814, *Daily Express*, 19 Jan. 1905.
31. Jeremy op. cit., pp.488–92; Besant; op. cit., pp.335–7.
32. D/B/BRY/1/2/622, Lucas, typescript, pp.87, 91; D/B/BRY/1/2/814, 5 Dec. 1908, *Liverpool Courier*, 8 Oct. 1910; *The Treasury*, June 1915, pp.244–9.
33. The NUGGL was the re-named gas-stokers' union founded in 1889. It merged with other societies to form the National Union of General and Municipal Workers in 1924.
34. *East End News & London Shipping Chronicle,*, 11 June 1912, p.1; and 14 June 1912, p.1; D/B/BRY/1/2/815, *Nottingham Guardian*, 11 Jan. 1912; *East End News*, 11 June 1912; *Daily Herald*, 8 June 1912; *Daily News*, 8 June 1912; D/B/BRY/1/2/628, draft article, 29 Oct. 1969.

35. D/B/BRY/1/2/544, *Brymay Pension Fund*; *Brymay Magazine*, June 1922, pp.185–7.
36. Even in 1925, 90–95 per cent of workers were in trades unions, predominantly the National Union of General and Municipal Workers, and the Workers Union. See LAB/2/1170/IR217/3/1925, Memo: Match Making Industry, 12 June 1925.
37. D/B/BRY/1/2/622, Lucas, typescript, pp.100, 118.
38. *Brymay Magazine*, June 1922, p.187; March 1929, p.112; LAB/2/960/IR274/4/23, Match Making JIC, Memos on Works Committees, 30 May 1923; 28 Dec. 1923; D/B/BRY/1/2/519, Fairfield Works Committee, 15 Nov. 1918; 7 Jan. 1919; 4 Feb. 1919; 1 April 1919; 1 July 1919; 29 July 1919; 2 Dec. 1919. Time-keeping remained a matter of concern throughout the 1920s, but showed a gradual improvement. See ibid., 4 April 1923; D/B/BRY/1/2/520, 7 April 1925; 3 April 1928; 7 July 1931; 5 April 1931; D/B/BRY/1/2/521, 2 Jan. 1934; 7 July 1938.
39. D/B/BRY/1/2/519, Fairfield Works Committee, 3 Feb. 1920; D/B/ BRY/1/2/622, Lucas, typescript, pp.100–10; *Brymay Magazine*, Dec. 1921, p.1; D/B/BRY/1/3/6, *General Meetings of Copartnership Trust Limited; Unity*, June 1928, pp.196–8.
40. D/B/BRY/1/2/622, Lucas, typescript, pp.102; *Brymay Magazine*, Nov. 1921, p.25; *Unity*, June 1928, p.197. By the 1920s, male staff had to insure their families in a contributory life policy. See D/B/BRY/1/3/19, *Brymay Copartnership, Also Provident Schemes and Welfare Organisation* (revised 1939), p.10.
41. D/B/BRY/1/2/519, Fairfield Works Committee, 4 Feb. 1919; 4 March 1919; 1 April 1919.
42. *Brymay Magazine*, Nov 1921, p.25; Jan. 1929, p.57; D/B/BRY/1/3/19, *Brymay Copartnership* . . ., p.9; D/B/BRY/1/3/3, Copartnership Trust Ltd, Committee of Management, 10 June 1920; 22 June 1921; 5 July 1922; 28 Feb. 1923; 20 June 1923; 19 Dec. 1927; 25 June 1930; 19 June 1935; 14 June 1939.
43. Brymay Magazine, Oct. 1921, p.1; Oct. 1921, pp.6–7, 10–16; Dec. 1921, pp.42, 67, 72; Jan. 1923, pp.83, 174; July 1924, p.233; Nov. 1928, pp.22, 35; D/B/BRY/1/2/519, Fairfield Works Committee, 5 June 1923; D/B/BRY/1/2/638, *The Brymay Book*, p.35, 37, 39, 41; D/B/BRY/1/3/35, *Bryant and May Savings Bank: Analysis of Balances, 1926–1972*.
44. *Brymay Magazine*, July 1922, p.208; July 1924, p.233; June 1927, p.189.
45. D/B/BRY/1/2/519, Fairfield Works Committee, 1 April 1919; 7 Feb. 1922; 7 March 1922; 6 Feb. 1923; D/B/BRY/1/3/19, *Brymay Copartnership* . . ., p.10; D/B/BRY/1/2/638, *The Brymay Book* (n.d.), p.45; D/B/BRY/1/3/3, Minutes of Committee of Management, 24 June 1931.
46. D/B/BRY/1/3/19, *Brymay Copartnership* . . ., p.11; *Brymay Magazine*, June 1922, p.185; LAB2/835/IR570/6/21, Match Making JIC, Supplementary Unemployment Benefit Scheme, pp.5–6 (1921). By 1934, the scheme had accrued £25,000 in reserves.
47. *Brymay Magazine*, Nov. 1921, p.17; June 1922, pp.184, 189–90; Jan. 1923, pp.172–3; June 1926, p.1; Jan 1929, pp.54–5; *East London Advertiser*, 21 May 1924, p.4; D/B/ BRY/1/2/622, Lucas op. cit., pp.102, 118; D/B/BRY/1/2/638, *The Brymay Book*, pp.33–4.
48. *Brymay Magazine*, June 1922, p.190; Jan. 1929, p.57; *Unity*, June 1928, p.196.
49. *Brymay Magazine*, Sept. 1924, p.1; April 1929, p.126; Dec. 1929, p.38; June 1931, pp.157–163.
50. See J. Child, 'Quaker Employers and Industrial Relations', *Sociological Review*, Vol.12 (1964), pp.293–315.
51. *Morning Advertiser*, 1 Aug. 1888, pp.5–6.

'SQUEEZING THE PULPLESS ORANGE': LABOUR AND CAPITAL ON THE RAILWAYS IN THE INTER-WAR YEARS

By GERALD CROMPTON

The railways figured prominently in the economic and political clashes which preceded and followed the First World War. Whilst they were still under state control, a major trial of strength between unions and government took place in 1919. Having been serious candidates for nationalisation, they were eventually reorganised by the Railways Act of 1921. With the aim of establishing a new balance between capital, labour and consumers, ownership was rationalised into four main companies, and new multi-level bargaining machinery was established on Whitley lines. This comprehensive settlement facilitated an early transition to conditions of stability in industrial relations. Despite the financially-damaging interruption of the General Strike in 1926, the first decade under the new post-war framework was characterised by effective collaboration between unions and management. But 1931, when general pay cuts were imposed for the second time, proved to be a watershed. Subsequently the same, much-admired bargaining institutions (subject to the modification of the top level in 1934) yielded far less acceptable results to the two parties. Conflict remained for the most part latent, but was contained with increasing difficulty until 1939. Although ridden with anxiety and uncertainty, the situation in the late 1930s was not altogether lacking in balance. Both sides had clear grounds for dissatisfaction: both were conscious of weakness and vulnerability. This paper examines the development of an increasingly tense relationship between railway companies and unions in the context of the multiple constraints affecting the industry as a whole.

The railway unions had made major advances during the period of government control between 1914 and 1921. The guaranteed eight-hour day and the guaranteed week had been obtained in 1919, and a week's paid holiday in 1920. Secure recognition was confirmed by the legislation of 1921 which gave statutory force to a set of both local and national bargaining arrangements, some of them already in operation. Although incorporated in legislation, this system was 'of a voluntary nature'. The peak level body, the National Wages Board (NWB), which employed quasi-judicial procedures, with formal representation of outside interests, could be regarded as 'really an arbitration tribunal'.[1] Another view was that it 'broke down the traditional distinction between arbitration and conciliation'. The same observer judged confidently at the end of the 1920s that 'an excellent spirit of accommodation' had prevailed there, with both sides 'willing to make reasonable adjustments'.[2] One of those most involved in its construction commented in 1925 that 'whilst there is no such thing as an absolute guarantee against disputes and strikes in industry, so far as that guarantee can be given there is no doubt it exists under the new railway machinery'. He also believed it conferred a 'new status' on the worker, who was no longer merely 'a hewer of wood and drawer of water', but 'now has a share in the responsibility for the conduct and management of the railways'.[3] Curiously, this exalted conception of the rights and duties of the employee had been the object of the proposals to give the unions seats on company boards which had been dropped in favour of the scheme actually adopted in 1921. But in any case such thinking heavily coloured the outlook of the National Union of Railwaymen under Thomas' leadership.

Early in 1920 the principle of a limited sliding scale for wages, subject to a base rate for each grade, was finally accepted, after strong opposition from within the NUR. It remained unpopular for a short time after its inception. Whilst prices were rising, wages followed them upwards rather more slowly, but then wages declined more slowly than the cost of living from late 1920 onwards. As prices fell, the higher-paid grades reached their base rate sooner, at a higher point on the cost of living index, and their wages were no longer subject to automatic adjustment. But a varying number of the lower-paid continued to receive some measure of assistance from the operation of the sliding scale.[4] Thomas and other NUR leaders became fond of reminding members of the shrewdness of this deal, and of the fact that critics had once alleged that it would reduce pay to a 'fodder' basis.[5] Another advantageous development during the period of government control was the general pay increase conceded in mid-1920 near the peak of post-war inflation. This was obtained on comparative rather than cost-of-living grounds. The Board recommended that the new level should not be disturbed 'for such a period as would facilitate a return to that stability of industry which is so necessary to the well-being of the community'.[6] Although not a permanent part of the post-war settlement, this rise could be interpreted as a lagged recognition of the effectiveness of the strike action taken in September 1919. It continued in operation for approximately two years.

Some ambiguities were persistent. One concerned the status of the standard rates of pay adopted early in 1920, on the basis of percentages (at least 100) above the pre-war figures. Some official statements, including a 1919 white paper, had implied that the new standards were intended to be permanent minima, subject to variation in an upward direction only. The opposing view was that these rates had no statutory sanction, although the subject of government agreement at the time, and were not irrevocable. They could be flexible downwards also.[7] The unions were never able to make their interpretation stick, but did succeed in investing the standard rates with a certain degree of legitimacy. In 1933 the chairman of the NWB, recommending cuts of around six per cent when the companies were pressing for ten per cent, denied that the rates were

strictly 'irreducible minima'. He did, however, accept that they had been
agreed as permanent standards, departure from which could be justified
only for strong reasons.[8]

Throughout the 1920s railway workers were conscious of enjoying
greatly improved living standards and working conditions by comparison
with the admittedly unsatisfactory pre-war situation. They were also
aware of having retained more of their war-related gains than their
counterparts in other trades, having avoided any major defeat in the
early 1920s. It was a realistic boast by the NUR general secretary in
1924 that 'we have held our corner up better than any other great
industry throughout the land'.[9] There had, of course, been some dis-
appointments, such as the failure to make any headway with the 'all
grades' programme of improvements in 1924–25, but any deterioration
in pay and conditions seemed marginal to most employees until the end
of the decade. The main setbacks were the institution of 'spread-over'
to nine or ten hours instead of the strict eight-hour day in 1922, the
reduction of mileage payments for locomen in 1924, and the withdrawal
of the war bonus for new entrants in 1926. Against this, the NWB had
on more than one occasion shown its value as a protective mechanism
by rejecting more serious management attacks on conditions (1923 and
1925). Although it required constant vigilance, this successful defensive
operation was appreciated all the more in the light of strong and well-
publicised pressure from outside the industry for the reduction of railway
wages and transport costs. In the circumstances the prestige of the three
main unions and their leaders was high, and they were able to draw on
a large reservoir of loyalty from members who had benefitted from the
achievements of their organisation, both offensive, and (increasingly)
defensive. The NUR in particular was highly committed to the success
of the new bargaining machinery and developed a strong and distinctive
leadership. It was able with surprising ease to rebuff internal criticism,
on both economic and political grounds, with the aid of the dominance
which Thomas, the political general secretary, usually exercised over the
union's conferences.

In 1928 the railways suffered a serious decline in freight receipts (probably attributable more to the current problems of heavy industry than to
intensification of road competition), and in the summer approached the
unions with a radical package of economy measures. Direct negotiations
yielded a two per cent pay cut. Not surprisingly, this was judged 'one
of the most remarkable agreements which have ever been effected in
the labour field'.[10] Thomas, with customary braggadocio, said it was 'a
lesson to the world . . . the best ever made'.[11] Indeed the principle of
a two per cent reduction for all, including managers and directors, was
suggested by the union side, and was considered essential to induce the
employers to withdraw demands not only for a bigger cut (originally five
per cent) but also for the abolition of the sliding-scale war bonus, of
enhanced payment for night and overtime work, and of the guaranteed
day. Such proposals would have fallen 'monstrously unfairly' on the

lower-paid sections of the membership and threatened 'the principles which it took years to obtain'.[12] In these circumstances, a limited concession on wages, with the union defences left intact on all other fronts, could be presented as a successful exercise in damage limitation. The 77–2 vote in favour of acceptance at an NUR delegate conference was the most spectacular example of Thomas' personal influence over his own organisation. His techniques of persuasion included alarmist references to declining union membership, denunciation of the strike alternative as 'madness', and the public reflection that 'if the railways go under we shall go under with them'.[13] There had been anxiety to avoid the danger of reference to the NWB, which might have upheld some or all of the companies' original proposals.[14] But if this tactic succeeded in 1928, it rebounded against the unions in 1936, when a company spokesman argued that net revenue was less than it had been eight years earlier when the unions had voluntarily accepted that their employers needed relief.[15]

The short-term response from railway workers was muted. There were complaints that management might have anticipated the emerging problem sooner, and worries that the cuts might be evaded by senior staff. Some thought the lower-paid should have been exempted altogether. A more radical view was that cuts should have been resisted as long as dividends were still being paid on watered capital, and as long as the companies retained large reserves.[16] On the other hand, the original management proposals attracted some sympathy from outside the railways. The guaranteed day was seen as imposing excessive rigidity, as the staff at many country stations allegedly did less than four hours' work in an eight-hour day. The deal was an example of 'practical altruism' in that some employees who fully earned their wages had made sacrifices in favour of others who did not.[17]

After the alarms of mid-1928, the financial situation of the industry improved quite rapidly. A year later *The Economist* was welcoming dividend statements as 'a welcome gleam of sunshine'.[18] Savings on wages, although only part of total reductions in expenditure, were almost equivalent to dividend increases to ordinary stockholders in 1929. On the LMSR, although gross revenues failed to rise, almost £1 million extra was distributed to shareowners, and this amount was more than covered by savings on pay.[19] Another perspective on the 1928 cuts was provided by a historically-minded article in the NUR journal early the following year. It described the 'reduction of 6d. in the pound' as 'not very material'. On the basis of wage and price changes since 1914 (when the author thought wages were too low), management would have had a case for cuts of more than four shillings in the pound.[20] The two per cent was restored in 1930.

For their part the railway companies, having survived the turbulence of the early post-war years, could look forward in the 1920s to reaching the levels of net revenue specified by the 1921 Act, as the benefits of amalgamation were gradually realised. Competition from road transport, especially for shorter distance passenger traffic, was already serious, but the prognosis was by no means hopeless. The evident necessity to reduce working costs emphasised the desirability of a positive relationship with authoritative union leaders in order to secure the collaboration of employees. In any case a rupture with organised labour was not a contingency which could be taken lightly at any time after the war. The worst outcome, a national strike, had the capacity to inflict virtually unlimited damage, and the events of 1919 and 1926 left it impossible to doubt that in certain circumstances, no doubt abnormal, but not easily predictable, the unions could find the requisite will and organisation. Almost any strike on the railways would quickly result in loss of revenue, whilst many heavy fixed costs remained. Interruption of services, apart from direct losses, carried an increasing danger of accelerating the seepage of traffic from rail to the largely non-union road sector. Below the level of possible national disputes, localised unofficial action served as a reminder that there were less tractable alternatives to the established trade union leaderships, and that the latter might not always be able to maintain control of their members if excessive pressure were placed on them. Furthermore the four railway groups, already highly-regulated oligopolies laden with the implicit duties of a public utility role, were ever sensitive to the publicity which their actions attracted and of the need for parliamentary and public approval. Any failure or loss of control on the part of railway management, whether in industrial relations or elsewhere, implied some threat to their future autonomy, via unfavourable regulation or increased government control.

An episode at the time of the General Strike illustrates both the caution of the railway leadership and the value they attached to preservation of the bargaining machinery. A director of one of the London underground concerns wrote to the Railway Companies Association to suggest that in order to facilitate a reduction of labour costs and of charges, strikers should be re-engaged on new terms 'on the clear understanding that all previous agreements are cancelled'. He suggested 10–15 per cent pay cuts, and lower overtime premiums, with reconsideration of the guaranteed day and week. The reply was that advice suggested that the strike had not cancelled the agreements and other arrangements under part IV of the Railway Act, and that the employers could not legally vary them except through the wage boards. It was also pointed out that the General Strike had itself been partly caused by assertions that any cut in miners' wages would be a signal for reductions in other industries. Therefore it would be 'extremely shortsighted and ill-advised for the companies now to take a line of action which would be seized upon by the extremists in the country as conclusive evidence of a conspiracy to reduce wages'.[21] Railway management, even though angered by a strike contrary to procedure, and determined to compel the unions formally to admit a 'wrongful act', was still anxious to uphold the machinery, and concerned to avoid provocations which might rekindle militancy.

Furthermore, although sometimes depicted as uncomfortably situated between the opposing forces of employees and shareowners, railway managers persisted in the belief that they could communicate with both, and persuade them of their common dependence on the prosperity of the industry. 'The interests of both parties are fundamentally identical',[22] insisted the *GWR Magazine* in 1934, deploring an outbreak of public controversy. In particular it was sometimes assumed that employers who had behaved reasonably could retain the loyalty of their own workers even when union leaders were not willing to co-operate. 'We have a loyal and contented staff',[23] the chairman of the GWR asserted implausibly, in the course of rebuking the unions for refusing to accept further pay cuts. This paternalist attitude was expressed less diplomatically by a general manager at the NWB who remarked 'I don't think they [the railway workers] understand much about finance'.[24]

In the 1930s most of the factors which had promoted stability since the early 1920s ceased to apply, or lost much of their potency. Reductions of around 4¾ per cent were implemented in mid-1931. A bid by the companies in 1932–33 to replace these with ten per cent cuts resulted in the fragmentation of the pay board, and its eventual reconstitution as the Railway Staff National Tribunal. The chairman had issued a single-handed recommendation for slightly increased reductions, but his authority was no longer acceptable to the unions. As the ASLEF leader Bromley put it, his men were beginning to regard the NWB 'not so much as a really impartial body . . . but as an instrument charged with a kind of electricity which it is very dangerous to us to touch'.[25] Management declined to enforce the chairman's decision unilaterally: to have done so would have invited an official strike. Railway pay was now lagging behind the average, especially once the general upward movement of money wages and prices was under way from 1934 onwards. In that year, however, a left-wing source acknowledged that 'in general the average level of earnings of those railwaymen still left in employment has been surprisingly well maintained, the drop of only 2 or 3 per cent between 1931 and 1934 being a striking tribute to the strength of railway trade unionism'.[26] But in the four years of railway recovery from 1933 to 1937, average earnings rose by an estimated 4.7 per cent, against a 12 per cent rise in the cost of living.[27]

It was obvious that the railways were not sharing fully in the expansion of the national economy. The fact that it took six years to achieve full restoration of the 1931 cuts acted as a running reminder that railway workers were not faring so well as in the recent past. The renewed economic downturn of 1938 hit the railways harder than most sectors, and in the last months of that year they became the first major industry to threaten absolute reductions in pay since the depression had begun to lift in 1933. Firm resistance to pay claims continued well into 1939, until the recovery in receipts was an accomplished fact, ensuring that the last year of peace would be one of recurring friction on the railways. The second half of the 1930s was, in comparative terms, the worst phase of the inter-war period for railway employees. Even so, figures cited by management to the RSNT in early 1939 showed that adult male manual workers were receiving 124 per cent (rates) and 140 per cent (earnings) more than before the war, representing an improvement of 45 per cent and 54 per cent respectively in real terms. Salaries were 97.7 per cent above pre-war levels, or 28 per cent in real terms. The white-collar employees, after experiencing a squeezing of their differentials during the war, had however, recovered some of the lost ground since 1920.[28]

But for most railway workers the terms of the pay-effort bargain seemed to have changed appreciably in the 1930s. The 'economania'[29] of their employers was experienced in a widespread deterioration of conditions. Among the problems which had to be faced were the extension of partial payment by results systems (some bonus element in earnings related to mileage travelled, or tonnage handled), the increased employment of young workers, partly at the expense of those in adult grades, greater use of seasonal and casual workers, the 'de-grading' of jobs (a given task being carried out by employees in a lower classification than previously), and the blocking of promotion opportunities, with the practice of 'putting back' (effectively, temporary demotion for an unspecified period) from higher to lower paid work. The context of these changes was a decline in the size of the labour force of about 200,000 between 1921 and the low point in 1933.

At the sharp end of the productivity offensive were those who came to fear the visits of the 'economy men' or the 'razor gang'.[30] Whether or not specific initiatives came from head office, it was clear that the exercise of managerial rights in the localities (often not contestable or negotiable through the official machinery) became a major source of economies for the companies and of insecurity for many employees. A rank and file publication, which often recorded the detailed consequences of the process, gave such examples as a list of 30 'passed' cleaners from the LMSR depot at Toton being transferred to other, and often distant, parts of the group's territory. Each was identified by initials, with brief details of family circumstances. It also reported that at Cricklewood, during a six-day period, over 1,000 hours of overtime were worked by footplate staff despite the fact that 'put-back' drivers and firemen were firing and cleaning respectively, and cleaners with twelve years' service were still cleaning.[31] So many different grades, both manual and white collar, were adversely affected by aspects of the attack on conditions, that a negative impact on staff morale was increasingly apparent. Commentators sympathetic to railway management thought it obvious by 1938 that 'ten years of cuts and rigid economies'[32] were showing their effects. When net receipts began to rise again from 1933, this was recognised, often with resentment, as partly the result of 'unrewarded intensification'[33] of their own labour by railway workers. Whereas in the 1920s any encroachment on existing standards and conditions might well be attributed to the effects of a temporary fall in demand, intensified by pressure from outside the industry, it now looked as though the railways themselves were committed to virtually continuous and relentless rationalisation. Of course this strategy was not optional for companies which had to cope with a combination of general economic depression and increased competition from the roads. Seen from a different angle, it was perhaps their most impressive achievement to reduce working costs almost in line with falling receipts through the late 1920s and early 1930s, and thereafter to contain the increase below the general level of inflation. This success overturned one of the established orthodoxies of the 1920s which held that a high proportion of railway costs was more or less fixed, and could not be scaled down if traffic or receipts declined.

The fall in net revenue to a trough in 1932 and the obvious competitive decline encouraged the balance of opinion to move, slowly and erratically, away from a view of the railways as 'sheltered' or privileged. But the moral pointed to wage earners remained remarkable similar. Either they were told that pay cuts would 'help to reduce the disequilibrium between sheltered and unsheltered trades'[34] – or they were exhorted to share the burden of depression with their employers on the grounds that railways had 'ceased to be a sheltered industry'.[35] It was no more helpful to point out that more pay might mean fewer jobs. NUR members were vividly reminded, when contemplating restoration of the 1928 cuts, that 'the squeezing of a pulpless orange is an unprofitable endeavour'.[36] But there was never any clear-cut trade-off available between pay and jobs or conditions. The railways were always more likely to make financial progress by cutting expenditure than by increasing gross receipts, and cost of all kinds were simultaneously targeted. The rising costs of materials was at least as worrying as wage pressure during the recovery of 1936 and 1937. Conflict over the level of pay may well have been more easily contained because the wage bill could be trimmed by reducing employment, mainly by non-replacement of leavers. In March 1933, for example, average weekly earnings were higher than twelve months earlier, largely because of overtime, but the companies enjoyed substantially lower labour costs because of a fall of more than 31,000 in numbers. Then an improvement in traffic later in 1933 necessitated an increase in staff, which had risen again by March 1934.[37] None of these fluctuations could have been anticipated with confidence.

Despite high levels of dissatisfaction on both sides, and several near-misses, only three major strikes took place in the inter-war years (1919, 1924, 1926), and the last of these was essentially external in origin. But on at least eighteen occasions between the General Strike and the Second World War, industrial action on the railways was recorded by the Ministry of Labour, and the list is undoubtedly incomplete.[38] The scale was generally small, and all the disputes were unofficial, and either unsupported, or actively opposed by the unions. Several did, nonetheless, show a tendency to spread from the focal point to neighbouring depots and stations. They mainly affected NUR members in large towns, with London especially prominent. Issues included the introduction of new, and more anti-social, duty rosters; methods of keeping work records; the treatment of young workers, especially the practice of either dismissing them or putting them on casual work when they reached the age of 20; staffing levels on railway vans; the dismissal of individuals and questions of promotion and outside appointments. The results of these protests varied: some failed, but there were successes too, and others were compromised.

In some cases local unofficial action was clearly related to national issues or principles. In March 1931 employees of all groups in London took 'go slow' action (leading to selective lock-outs of those who failed to give assurances of normal working) in protest against the recent wage-cutting decision of the NWB. An additional related objective was to obtain guarantees that the extended 'spread-over' of the working day for up to 12 hours would not be applied in London. The NUR intervened to prevent the spread of the action, arguing that acceptance of the NWB decision was the only alternative to a 'serious and disastrous dispute'.[39]

The biggest railway dispute of the 1930s also took place in London, in October 1938. It grew out of a 'show cards' campaign – a drive for 100 per cent membership – and began with the refusal of 300 ticket collectors and porters at St. Pancras to work with a non-unionist who had lapsed from the NUR after the General Strike. The strike spread to at least eight other stations and depots, and eventually caused the loss, according to Ministry figures, of 12,500 working days over a six-day period. This unauthorised action was predictably denounced by the union as 'seriously prejudicial to the interests of the organisation as a whole'.[40] Ironically, 100 per cent membership, and the elimination of the 'nons' was an aim traditionally common to both the union leadership and its most radical critics. Some of Thomas' speeches at the time of the 1928 negotiations had included scathing attacks on non-unionists.[41]

The limited successes achieved by unofficial action suggest that strong workplace organisation, especially in the larger stations and depots, could have some impact on a range of issues concerning the application of national agreements, seniority, rostering and staffing levels. Sometimes progress was possible through official channels, mainly the Local Department Committees, the lowest level of the bargaining machinery, despite much scepticism among union members about their high failure rate ('"Deferred for enquiry", "not conceded", "outside the scope of the machinery" – what railwayman has not these automatic decisions off by heart?').[42] The foundation of the Railwaymen's Vigilance Movement in 1933 encouraged the formulation and expression of grievances in the workplace and provided a degree of co-ordination for militants, a programme of demands, and a focus for opposition to current union leadership. It enjoyed more credibility than its predecessor, the Railwaymen's Minority Movement, because it had dropped the previous insistence on the independent leadership of the Communist Party and on the strategy of trying to organise all-grades shed and depot committees outside the existing union structure. The Vigilance Movement was able to establish a presence in a number of branches and workplaces, and to advance some of its active members within the organisation of the unions.[43]

The NUR leadership in the 1930s was a good deal less cohesive and self-confident than in the 1920s, and was obliged to pay more attention to members' grievances, which were not, however easily rectified. Fears for the future of the industry and consciousness of the threat from the largely unorganised road haulage sector was certainly an inhibiting factor. ('We have been talking about a 36-hour week for railwaymen. I have come across fellows who are working 36 hours at a stretch on lorries').[44] The NWB decision of 1931 contained a minor but chilling irony – the only section of the NUR membership to receive any advance was the crossing-keepers who were deemed worthy of extra payment because of heavier traffic on the roads.

A hesitant approach to possible conflict had several sources. The General Strike had had a long-lasting effect on union finances, there were often well-founded doubts about the prospects for inter-union agreement, and also worries about the morale of union members. In the NUR other influences derived from some central aspects of the union's own tradition. Its leaders had worked long and hard to reinforce the legitimacy of the industry's bargaining machinery, and to discourage any spontaneous or unofficial action. In a characteristic metaphor of Thomas', 'they must play cricket with the owners if they expected the owners to play cricket with them'.[45] Disaster, for union, or industry, or country was often predicted as the consequence of a possible strike. The NUR's next most influential leader, Cramp, who remained general secretary until 1933, liked to commend 'the exercise of human intelligence' in contrast to striking, which 'cannot win for us permanent prosperity'. By way of criticism of ASLEF, he explained that 'so far as the NUR is concerned we are going to base our progress on the processes of the brain and make negotiations a science'.[46]

Although union leaders had themselves made a weighty contribution to weakening combativity, lack of confidence among the membership was often invoked to justify acceptance of unfavourable and unpopular settlements. 'I felt the men were not ready for a struggle',[47] explained the NUR president, with reference to the 1931 cuts. His successor, at the pre-conference meeting in 1937, expressed confidence in the justice of the pending claim, and in the ability of their spokesman at the Tribunal, trusting that satisfaction could be secured by 'reasoned argument and persuasion', but warned that responsibility for accepting or rejecting the decision rested with the members.[48] Indecisiveness could also afflict delegate bodies. An NUR special conference in May 1936 negatived both a resolution to accept the companies' offer and also another one to call a strike if no improvement were obtained. In early 1939 the executives of all three unions rejected tribunal awards, and in the space of a few months two unions decided only by very narrow majorities against striking. ASLEF did finally call a strike in the summer, but was then dissuaded from proceeding because of the imminence of war. At other times the key factor was caution rather than indecisiveness, with a clear gap emerging between delegates' attitudes and their will to implement the action which was logically implied. An ASLEF conference called the 1931 cuts 'monstrous', and decided to accept them.[49] Again in January 1937 the same union rejected a tribunal report by a large majority, but failed to impose sanctions. Prudence may on occasion have escalated to such heights as to obscure self-interest. The NUR's historian plausibly suggests that in 1934 a further direct approach to the companies might have resulted in a better settlement. Such lack of forcefulness could have been a by-product of the moderation of the original claim for restoration of cuts. Sharp dissatisfaction coexisted with the feeling, expressed in 1936, that striking was not worthwhile when the difference was 'all over the price of a packet of cigarettes'.[50]

The railway unions, though marginally fewer than the grouped companies, found it harder to achieve unity in action. The most serious areas of competitive recruitment were between the NUR and ASLEF, with most success going to the latter. The weakest areas of union organisation were among the lower grades of manual workers and the higher grades of white collar staff. It was unfortunate that the strongest and most cohesive group of railway employees, the locomen, belonged in the main to an organisation constituted on sectional lines. Although solidarity developed powerfully at times of heightened trade union activity (1919 and 1926), relations between the two major manual unions were frequently sour. One of the worst phases followed the 1924 locomen's strike, when ASLEF's separate action met the active disapproval of the NUR. This was fuelled by a sense of outrage that ASLEF had rejected an NWB report which had been signed by their own representatives. Instead they had struck, after a membership ballot which favoured that course by 6-1. An NUR circular described this as 'a blow at the very principle of collective bargaining', and reminded members, urging them to work normally, 'that the honour and prestige of their union is at stake'.[51] By 1933 the NUR leadership had of course acquired a different perspective on the sanctity of NWB decisions. The strike apparently achieved little more than delay in the application of reduced mileage payments, but a substantive concession (not claimed by the NUR) was obtained from the wages board at the end of 1924.[52] ASLEF not surprisingly, did not then join an unsuccessful claim by the two other unions for their all-grades programme.

In 1931 any possibility of resistance to the general pay cuts was limited by the fact that ASLEF, which had been granted a small increase for cleaners and shunter drivers, accepted before the NUR. In 1936 ASLEF submitted an ambitious separate claim to RSNT, without success, but in 1937 joined the other unions to achieve the final restoration of the 1931 cuts in addition to pursuing its own objectives. 1938 again saw a failure to present common claims, although in 1939 the RCA threw its weight behind the central NUR aim of a 50 shillings minimum rate. These splits allowed a company advocate to point the obvious contrast between the unions' policy commitment to the national co-ordination of transport, and their inability to harmonise their own bargaining aims.[53]

Apart from crucial failures to support each other during actual or potential disputes, inter-union differences also reflected varying problems and priorities. ASLEF's self-image was presented clearly to one wages board as that of 'a good class of men who had worked very earnestly to fit themselves for their jobs'.[54] In the mid- and late 1930s they concentrated largely on issues of rosters, hours and holidays. Their spokesmen emphasised 'the mental strain of enginemen',[55] involving the increased variety of signalling systems, the weight of locomotives and length of trains, and the general speed-up. They also complained that promotion in pre-grouping days took effect 'ten to twelve years earlier than was the case today'.[56] The RCA, which had similar concerns, produced figures in 1937 to show that 12,798 male clerks, out of 55,036 members, were 'stagnating', having spent at least three years at the top of their pay scale – partly because of a considerable drop in the number of positions above class 5. But their bid for a £10 p.a. increase for clerks in this situation was turned down, with management claiming the problem was 'inherent in the classification arrangements'.[57] A simultaneous claim for a 36-hour week was rejected by the tribunal, and criticised as 'extravagantly conceived'.

The NUR, in contrast, focussed increasingly on the target of a 50 shillings adult minimum wage. Existing rates were judged inadequate to provide the necessaries of life, and many members had to accept an 'existence' rather than a 'comfort' standard. A series of household budgets compiled by members and their families was submitted to tribunals, and the results compared with the dietaries set out by Seebohm Rowntree in his study of 'The Human Needs of Labour'. The cost of Rowntree's minimum dietary was greater than the 'meagre earnings of many railwaymen could afford'. In the summer of 1937 about 100,000 railwaymen had basic rates below 50 shillings a week, though as the companies stressed, the number fell to about 68,000 in terms of earnings.[58] To prioritise the needs of the lowest paid made sense to the NUR, partly because claims on this basis were most likely to win sympathy, and because the cost of living had been rising faster than railway net revenue since 1934. Comparative arguments were also persuasive. In January 1939 it could be stated that out of 46 recent awards by trade boards, only three laid down rates below the railway minimum.[59] However attempts to raise the lowest rate evoked not only the objection of cost but also the counter-assertion that it would reduce differentials to such an extent as to 'destroy the relationship between the grades'. This was also denounced as 'standardisation run riot'.[60]

Fundamental issues were more often raised, but not easily solved, in the bargaining exchanges of the 1930s. The unions insisted that the first charge on revenue should be the payment of adequate wages to those who had 'invested their lives and their earning power in the industry.' Asked what he meant by 'a high percentage of dividend', an

NUR spokesman 'thought the percentage was always high if the men's conditions had to suffer . . . Anything in excess of 1 per cent was high. He did not agree with the shareholders getting anything.'[61]

The companies increasingly stressed the 'ability to pay' factor. In crises such as 1932–33 they were prepared to push their defensive case to extremes of self-denigration. They were 'a vital industry stricken to the point of exhaustion', they were suffering from 'a process of creeping paralysis, none the less fatal because it came gradually', via lack of credit and high costs. The issue of prior charge securities 'must in time overweight the financial structure'. On the other hand, 'not to issue capital would be fatal'.[62] As one unfriendly critic put it, 'railway capital masqueraded in the rags of a beggar'.[63]

The railways were unusual in that their stockholders were roughly as numerous as their employees. They were typically portrayed as 'men and women of slender means who ventured their small savings',[64] and much was made of the alleged hardships they suffered. The employers' advocate at the NWB in December 1932, pleading for a ten per cent wage cut, said he had three main arguments, of which the first was 'justice to the shareholders'.[65] But appeals for sympathy on these lines could provoke derisive references to the apparent predominance of 'widows and orphans' among railway stockholders.[66] The most detailed survey available of the distribution of stock, which was carried out in the early 1940s, found that it was even more skewed than elsewhere. Although large holdings were only a small fraction of the total, 'medium-sized holdings have greater importance, and the smallest holdings are correspondingly less prominent' than in other large companies.[67]

Much depended, of course on what type of investment had been made, and when. Those with fixed interest securities were an unusually large, and increasing, proportion of the total, and were sometimes said, enviously, to be 'on velvet',[68] especially during the long period of falling prices. Cumulative preference shares were also in a relatively protected position. But the top-heavy capital structure, and the competitive decline of the industry put the main burden of low net receipts on to the ordinary stockholders.[69] These formed an unhappy group, who went without dividends in the worst years, and seem to have experienced something akin to alienation from their own capital, which they felt was being effectively destroyed or confiscated as a result of various company or union policies of which they disapproved. For all kinds of stock, however, the date of purchase was crucial. Through most of the inter-war period the market price stood well below par, and those who had bought recently at low prices were enjoying higher yields than investors of longer standing. The wages board was told by the NUR spokesman in December 1932 that current prices implied an average return of just over 6 per cent on railway capital.[70] On the high-risk ordinary stock, the rewards could be much higher. In March 1930 it was noted that yields of eight-and-a-half per cent to nine-and-a-half per cent were currently obtainable, which was described as 'a range more appropriate to new and speculative "patent" or mining enterprises than to indispensable public utility concerns in a great industrial country'.[71] At the NWB in late 1932 evidence was presented from a sample of 1,275 blocks of LMSR ordinary stock to indicate that over the previous ten years the annual turnover by sale had been no more than about 2.6 per cent. The company 'did not ask for sympathy for rich shareholders or recent investors'.[72]

It became a permanent grievance that 'standard revenue', as defined in the 1921 Act, was never achieved. This would have implied an average return on nominal capital of around 4.7 per cent by the late 1930s. At the low point of depression in 1932, the actual rate had dipped as low as 2.59 per cent. In 1937 the returns were 3.9 per cent for debentures, 3.8 per cent for guaranteed and preference stock, and 1.46 per cent for ordinary. (Corresponding figures for a sample of 2,271 other companies estimated by *The Economist* in that year were 4.5 per cent, 5.4 per cent, and 9 per cent).[73] In the worst years of the early 1930s, over £300 million of railway capital had gone dividendless, and by 1939, the total sum 'lost' since 1931 was well over £100 million, (cumulative shortfall of interest and dividend below standard revenue). Equally strong evidence of deprivation was the marked shift in the balance of the net product of the industry away from capital and towards labour. An approximate 50–50 division in 1913 had become roughly 75–25 in favour of labour by the early 1930s.[74] Such a trend would of course be expected in any firm or industry in which profits had declined significantly. Some of capital's more radical critics denounced all transfers of surplus to shareowners as 'unpaid labour which is filched from railway workers by railway parasites'. (It was around 6s 7d in every pound in 1929).[75]

A more common objection to shareholder's complaints was that the capital stock contained a good deal of 'water' (usually calculated at something approaching 20 per cent).[76] The effect of discounting this water was to raise the apparent rate of return. In fact post-war railway capital contained relatively little 'water' in the normal sense of shares for which no money had ever been subscribed. However, there were good grounds for regarding the railways as over-capitalised by reason of inflated expenditure on their construction,[77] and because of irreversible decline in the earning capacity of their assets by the 1930s. One acid comment on the 1930 centenary was that 'the waste of capital in early railway development would be a good subject for a tableau'.[78] Many believed that 'the burden of unremunerative capital was imposing an earnings standard on the railways which has no relationship to railway economics at the present time'.[79] Despite the poor state of the industry in the early 1930s a glance at the records reminded critics that over the past decade some £500 million, about half the nominal capitalisation, had been distributed to stockholders, and that until recently an up-to-the-hilt dividend policy had prevailed.[80] Conversely, a common response from owners of shares was that wages, rather than dividends and interest, were higher than net revenue justified. Trade union claims were seen as threatening a fragile recovery in the late 1930s, and 'frightening investors away from railway stock'.[81]

Few constructive suggestions were put forward by organised share-owners.[82] Their preference for specialist, full-time directors, rather than part-timers with wide outside interests, was an implicit protest against the public utility role of the railways, and their subordination to the interest of capital in other sectors of the economy. Nor were the demands for a tougher line with the unions, or for a crack-down on expenditure likely to find favour with management. Such complaints did, however, force directors to spell out on several occasions the rationale, basically defensive, for spending limited amounts on carefully selected and costed capital projects.[83] There was of course no improvement in the credit rating of the railways, and additional capital could be raised only by issuing prior charge securities, which 'stood in front' of the ordinary stock.

By 1939 an increasingly unsatisfactory situation had developed in which arguably neither stockholders, employers, nor railway users could have much confidence in the future. The unions had for the most part operated within agreed procedures, had strongly discouraged unofficial action, and shown consistent concern for the economic situation of the industry. Yet the results for their members were declining relative pay (over the last five years), worsened conditions and damaged career prospects. Management could claim to have been operationally efficient, as the Railway Rates Tribunal annually testified, but was too hard-pressed financially either to reward its shareholders adequately, or to make essential investments. Directors were well-schooled in various public policy issues, and were currently engaged in negotiating a 'Square Deal' for the railways, including both some reduction in legal regulation, and greater co-operation with certain road haulage interests. But this strategy involved risks as well as opportunities, and optimism was limited. From the standpoint of government, legislation had already been passed in 1928, 1930 and 1933 to provide a measure of assistance to the railways, or of regulation for road transport. Those industries with higher unemployment or greater exposure to international competition remained more plausible candidates for possible government help or reorganisation. The financial problems of the railways, though real enough, were generally viewed as less severe than those of other sectors of the economy.[84] Nationalisation, state co-ordination of transport, or capital restructuring of the railways were all topics for sporadic public controversy rather than for the immediate political agenda. The upshot was a deep stalemate, reflecting the insolubility of railway problems within the existing structure of ownership and regulation.

University of East Anglia

NOTES

1. PRO LAB 2/767/10. Comment by G.H. Ince.
2. Lord Amulree, *Industrial Arbitration in Great Britain* (Oxford, London, 1929), p.167.
3. J.H. Thomas, 'Labour Organisation on British Railways', in J.R. Bailey *et al.*, *Modern Railway Administration, Vol.II* (London, 1925), p.234.
4. Just over 90,000 were in this category by March 1931, and only 13,416 by December 1932. The number rose again in the middle and late thirties as prices increased.
5. *Railway Review*, 22 June 1923.
6. PRO LAB 2/767/10. National Wages Board Report, June 1920.
7. PRO LAB 10/410. A Brief Industrial History of the Railways in Great Britain.
8. *Labour Research*, Feb. 1933.
9. *Railway Review*, 8 Feb. 1924.
10. *The Economist*, 4 Aug. 1928.
11. Quoted in S. Purkis, 'Danger Ahead', *Labour Monthly*, Nov. 1930. It was suggested that Thomas' achievement should be commemorated in an illuminated address, depicting a kneeling railway director in each corner, a top hat rampant in the top centre, and a coffin containing the all-grades programme in the bottom centre. *Workers' Life*, 17 Aug. 1928.
12. *Railway Review*, 27 June 1928 and 10 Aug. 1928.
13. Ibid., 20 July 1928.
14. A year later Cramp speculated publicly that the companies would probably have got 'about 50 per cent of what they asked for' at the NWB. *Railway Review*, 5 July 1929.
15. *Railway Gazette*, 3 July 1936.
16. *Monthly Circular of the Labour Research Department*, Sept. 1928.
17. *The Economist*, 4 Aug. 1928.
18. Ibid., 3 Aug. 1929.
19. Ibid., 1 March, 1930.
20. *Railway Review*, 4 Jan., 11 Jan., 18 Jan., 1929. Articles by F. Lees.
21. General Managers' Minutes, 11 May 1926. GWR. The General Strike, Vol.II. BRB Archive.
22. *GWR Magazine*, Oct. 1934.
23. *Railway Gazette*, 24 Feb. 1933.
24. Quoted on the cover of the pamphlet *The National Wages Board and After*, Labour Research Department (London, Jan. 1933).
25. Ibid., p.3.
26. W. Fox, *Seven Years of Railway Finance, 1928–34*, Labour Research Department (London, 1935).
27. See the pamphlet, *Justice for Railwaymen*, Labour Research Department (London, 1938) p.7.
28. *Railway Gazette*, 3 Feb. 1939.
29. A phrase used in *Railway Review*, 13 July 1928.
30. *Railway Vigilant*, March and Oct. 1933.
31. Ibid., May and Jan. 1933.
32. *The Economist*, 19 March 1938.
33. R. Hyman, 'Rank and File Movements and Workplace Organisation, 1914–39' in C.J. Wrigley (ed.), *A History of British Industrial Relations, Vol.2 1914–39* (Brighton, 1987), p.146.
34. *The Economist*, 17 Dec. 1932.
35. Ibid., 1 Nov. 1930.
36. Ibid., 13 July 1929.
37. *Labour Research*, Oct. 1933 and Nov. 1934.
38. PRO LAB 34/45–34/52.
39. *Labour Research*, May 1931. *Railway Gazette*, 13 March 1931.

40. *Labour Research*, Nov. 1938. PRO, LAB 34/52. Although the latter source categorises the strike as unsuccessful, the former (Feb. 1939) sums it up as 'fought successfully for 100 per cent trade unionism', implying that the non-unionist was transferred to some other station.
41. *Railway Review*, 27 July 1928.
42. Pamphlet, *The Railwaymen's Fight*, Railwaymen's Minority Movement (London, Sept. 1929), p.11.
43. The All-Grades Railwaymen's Vigilance Movement was formed at the beginning of 1933 and held a conference in London in January of that year which was attended by 147 delegates, 56 of them from the provinces.
44. *Daily Worker*, 7 July 1932.
45. *Railway Review*, 2 Nov. 1928.
46. Ibid., 8 Feb. 1924.
47. *Labour Research*, Dec. 1932.
48. *Railway Gazette*, 4 July 1937.
49. PRO, LAB 10/410. op. cit.
50. P.S. Bagwell, *The Railwaymen* (London, 1963), p.549.
51. *Monthly Circular of the Labour Research Department*, Feb. 1924.
52. PRO, LAB 10/410. op. cit.
53. Bagwell, op. cit., p.552.
54. *Railway Gazette*, 16 Dec. 1932.
55. Ibid., 23 July 1937.
56. Ibid., 3 Feb. 1939.
57. Ibid., 30 July 1937.
58. Ibid., 23 and 30 July 1937.
59. Bagwell, op. cit., p.559.
60. *Railway Gazette*, 7 July 1939.
61. Ibid., 23 July 1937 and 16 Dec. 1932.
62. Ibid., 2 Dec. 1932.
63. Pamphlet, *Rail Crisis* (Edinburgh, 1933).
64. C. Stuart-Williams and E. Short, *Railways, Roads and the Public* (London, 1939), p.120.
65. *Railway Gazette*, 23 Dec. 1932.
66. Pamphlet, *Wages and Profits on the Railways*, Labour Research Department (London, Dec. 1932).
67. 'Who Owns the Railways?'. Four articles by H.P. (H.R. Parkinson) *Financial News* 31 Oct, 1, 2, 3 Nov. 1944. Summarised in H. Parkinson, *Ownership of Industry* (London, 1951) p.63.
68. *The Railowner,* Feb. 1935.
69. By the autumn of 1939, a total capital stock of £1,100 million consisted of £315 million debentures, £145 million guaranteed and cumulative preference shares, £365 million other preference shares, and £275 million ordinary shares. *Railway Gazette*, 1 Sept. 1939.
70. Ibid., 9 Dec. 1932.
71. *The Economist*, 1 March 1930.
72. *Railway Gazette*, 9 Dec. and 23 Dec. 1932.
73. Cited in Stuart-Williams and Short, op. cit., p.122.
74. *Railway Gazette*, 30 July 1937.
75. *Rail Crisis*, op. cit., p.3.
76. W. Fox, *Ten Years of Railway Finance*, Labour Research Department (London, 1932), p.6, estimated 18.8 per cent of total capital was water in 1930.
77. R.J. Irving, 'The Capitalisation of Britain's Railways 1830–1914', *Journal of Transport History*, 3rd series, Vol.5 (1984).
78. *Labour Research*, Nov. 1930.
79. *Justice for Railwaymen*, op. cit.
80. *The Economist*, 9 March 1929.
81. *The Railway Stockholder*, Oct. 1938.

82. From 1933 the British Railway Stockholders' Union claimed to represent all those with a stake in railway capital, though holders of the ordinary stock seem to have been most active. It incorporated some of its predecessors, such as the Railway Reform League, and the LNER Stockholders' Association.
83. Statements by the Chairmen of the LNER and LMSR. *The Railowner,* Feb. 1935 and Dec. 1935 respectively.
84. These problems are discussed in G.W. Crompton, '"Efficient and Economical Working"? The Performance of the Railway Companies 1923–33', *Business History*, Vol.-XXVII, 2, (1985).

PRODUCT MARKETS, LABOUR MARKETS, AND INDUSTRIAL RELATIONS: THE CASE OF FLOUR MILLING

By HOWARD F. GOSPEL

Adam Smith was well aware of collusion between firms both in the product market and in the labour market. On the former he commented, 'The monopolists, by keeping the market constantly under-stocked, by never fully supplying the effectual demand, sell their commodities much above the natural price and raise their emoluments . . . greatly above their natural rate'.[1] On the latter he stated that 'Masters are always and everywhere in a sort of tacit, but constant and uniform combination, not to raise the wages of labour above their actual rate'.[2]

This article examines the interaction between employers' product market activities and their labour market strategies in one industry, flour milling, which, though small, provides an interesting example of the relationship between employers' commercial and industrial relations policies. Flour milling was also an industry which in the interwar years considered itself and was held by others to have developed a particularly comprehensive and exemplary system of industrial relations.[3] Having examined the formation of the industry's national system of industrial relations in the interwar period, the article then considers the trans-formation of that system in the post-Second World War history of the industry. It is hoped that the case study permits us to see the dynamics of interaction between changing product market structures and industrial relations.

The article also provides a perspective on the rise and decline of national collective bargaining in Britain. The standard interpretation, as best articulated by the Donovan Royal Commission and the Oxford School of Industrial Relations,[4] places paramount emphasis on factors endogenous to the industrial relations system and in particular on the role of the trade union. According to this perspective, union pressures in the late nineteenth and early twentieth centuries led to the growth of employers' organisations; the latter subsequently developed policies of collective containment which created national procedural and wage sys-tems; in the post-Second World War period, the emergence of informal workplace bargaining, stimulated by full employment and the growth of shop steward power, undermined the formal industry-wide system of negotiations; in order to contain this, in the 1960s and 1970s, employers developed new strategies based on plant- and company-bargaining. Such an account gives little prominence to the product market and commercial position of the employer which, it is argued here, were of central importance in shaping collective bargaining structures.

I

In the product market, collusive arrangements such as market sharing and price fixing had a long history in many British industries. In the final quarter of the nineteenth century, confronted by new competitive pressures and a threat to profit margins, there was a growth in trade associations and collusive practices.[5] During the First World War, encouraged by government controls and rationing, both formal associations and informal restrictive practices increased further.[6] As the 1918 Report of the Committee on Trusts stated, 'there is at the present time in every branch of industry in the UK an increasing tendency to the formation of trade associations and combinations, having for their purpose the restriction of competition and the control of prices'.[7] Depressed demand conditions in the early and late 1920s and in the early 1930s placed considerable strains on many trade associations, and some restrictive agreements collapsed. However this was often only an initial reaction to the appearance of excess capacity, and mutual adversity soon led to renewed collusion in many industries.[8] Thus in 1929 another government committee remarked on 'the tendency for separate productive undertakings to associate themselves with other enterprises with a view to regulating output, prices, machinery, and other matters'.[9] From the 1930s onwards there were additional factors which made such restrictive practices more effective. The merger wave and increase in concentration which occurred in the 1920s made it possible in some industries for a smaller number of larger firms to organise collusion.[10] The adoption of protection in 1932 reduced the threat of import competition and thus bolstered up restrictive arrangements in the home market. In addition government became more supportive in an attempt to help the rationalisation of industries such as shipbuilding and iron and steel. The restrictive arrangements which were created during the interwar years were to last into the immediate post-Second World War period.

In the labour market, employers' organisations also had a long history, and, again from the final quarter of the nineteenth century, there was an increase in their number and stability. At that time national associations were established in most major British industries, such as cotton, engineering, shipbuilding. At first some of these were fiercely anti-trade union and opposed collective bargaining. Later, however, they saw some advantages in recognising unions and entered into collective bargaining with them, establishing procedural arrangements for handling disputes and subsequently entering into agreements on wages and conditions. Before the First World War, however, collective bargaining in most industries was at workplace or district level, and wages and conditions agreements were largely *ad hoc* and limited in scope and effectiveness. During the war and in the immediate post-war years there was a considerable expansion of collective bargaining and a growth of more formal agreements at national level. These differed greatly in scope and effectiveness, but in most industries constituted the main formal medium of collective bargaining in the early post-Second World War period.

The system of collective bargaining in flour milling was particularly innovative and comprehensive.

The flour milling industry was transformed from the 1880s onwards by the introduction of automatic steel-roller milling which allowed wheat to be ground more efficiently than by traditional stone-grinding methods in wind- and water-mills. This led to the growth of large mills located at ports and using low-priced foreign wheats for year-round milling. Such highly mechanised firms gained economies of throughput and scale, grew in size, and sold their output in an expanding national market. Small and medium-sized mills, located in rural areas and inland towns, serving local farmers and markets, continued to exist but with a decreasing share of the market. In 1880 there were about 10,000 mills in Britain; by 1917 this number had been reduced to 1,000, of which about one quarter produced 90 per cent of total flour output.[11] By the First World War a number of firms had risen to prominence and grew further through internal expansion and acquisitions in the 1920s. By the late 1920s Ranks, Spillers, and the Cooperative Wholesale Society (CWS) between them were producing about two-thirds of UK flour.[12]

In 1878 the National Association of British and Irish Millers was established.[13] Before the First World War there were various attempts at output regulation and price-fixing on an area basis which tended to work for a time but then disintegrated.[14] During the war and up to September 1921, prices were controlled by the government and firms were guaranteed profits according to capacity. In these circumstances millers enjoyed prosperity and increased their output. The result was that after decontrol the industry faced a situation of excess capacity. This was accentuated throughout the inter-war period by an inelastic demand situation for, as real wages rose, the population increasingly changed to other foodstuffs.[15] These factors led in the 1920s to a period of fierce competition between millers which reduced profit margins in the industry.

In 1929 Ranks and Spillers, who by then controlled nearly half of the UK's milling capacity, took the initiative and along with other large firms in the industry set up the Millers' Mutual Association (MMA).[16] This highly secretive organisation covered most of the milling industry and was to have a considerable effect on its commercial fortunes and industrial structure. Under its constitution member firms were allocated a quota based on their previous three years' production and those which exceded their quota paid a premium to the Association. New mills could only be built within existing quotas or by purchasing extra quota rights. Where a firm could not sell its full quota in a particular year, compensation was paid from a central fund, but thereafter a new and lower quota pertained. Where firms were constantly unable to meet their quota, they could opt to be bought out by the Association. For this purpose a limited company, Purchase Finance Co. Ltd. was established, and seven shares issued, one to each of the largest firms in the industry. This company then bought up and closed down the weaker mills in the industry. Under these arrangements the country was divided up and uniform prices were fixed on an area basis. This price fixing was facilitated by the fact that the industry was not open to foreign competition: exports were very small, and imports, which had never been very important, were from 1932 onwards subject to a ten per cent *ad valorem* duty. In this way from 1929 onwards, though the price of wheat fell, the price of flour was maintained at a level which allowed good profits.[17] Because of their greater efficiency the largest firms benefitted most, grew in size, and increased their market share.

The total labour force of the industry was small, numbering about 50,000 in 1918. Of these about 40 per cent might be described as skilled mill workers.[18] Labour costs constituted about five per cent of the total costs.[19] However it must be remembered that the price of wheat represented about 70 per cent of the total cost of flour. If labour costs are taken as a proportion of the 'millers' margin' (the difference between the cost of wheat and the price of flour) then wages represented about 20 per cent.[20] Industrial relations in the industry had traditionally been good. In part this may have reflected a paternalism which had its origins in the rural location of many early mills,[21] but it was also because the industry offerred reasonably secure employment and many mill workers enjoyed a progression up a well defined hierarchy. Undoubtedly also good relations were encouraged in the interwar years by the policies to be described below.

Before the First World War there was little trade union organisation or collective bargaining in the industry. A National Union of Millers had established itself in London before the war, and during the war it spread throughout the country and increased its membership to about 10,000.[22] In 1920 this union, a Liverpool union, and a small Midlands mill workers' union joined with Ernest Bevin's Dockers' Union to form a part of the Transport and General Workers Union (TGWU), henceforward the largest union in the industry, representing about 80 per cent of employees.[23]

In 1918 a Labour Advisory Committee of the National Association of British and Irish Millers was formed which shortly after became the Flour Milling Employers' Federation (FMEF) with a separate existence and full-time staff. Three factors had combined to bring about the establishment of the Federation and its recognition of trade unions. First, following on the increase in union membership and the short- age of labour during the war, the various unions pursued a policy of leapfrogging wage claims between mills and areas. In order to contain this, employers in London and other areas combined together and negotiated wage schedules.[24] Second, government arbitration awards for the industry during and immediately after the war took the form of flat-rate across-the-board increases for the industry as a whole. These simultaneously narrowed differentials between firms and accustomed the industry to acting collectively in labour matters. As a result it was not surprising that when, after the war, the government declined to intervene further in industrial relations, the industry should have concluded its first voluntary agreement in February 1919.[25] Third, the employers, with a strong sense of their own industry identity, were already interested in the proposals of the Whitley Committee for industry-based councils to regulate industrial relations.[26] They felt it was better to institute their own arrangements rather than have them imposed by the government.[27]

FMEF membership was high, representing about 90 per cent of flour output, with non-federated firms being mainly small and located in rural areas.[28] The Federation was always concerned about non-membership because it feared wage-rate undercutting and it did not want to appear to be exclusively an organisation of large firms.[29] It did not wish to drive small firms out of the Federation because this would have negated one of the reasons for setting up the Federation, namely the introduction of order and predictability in both the labour and product market. Nevertheless a small number of large firms, led by Ranks and Spillers, always dominated the Federation's activities.

The establishment of the Federation induced reluctant firms to recognise trade unions because it put all firms in the same position and none were placed at a comparative disadvantage by granting recognition. Subsequently it pursued a twofold policy with regards to the unions. On the one hand it felt it desirable to recognise all the main unions in the industry 'in order that with competition in this direction power should not be concentrated in the hands of one union'.[30] At the same time, however, it insisted on bargaining with all the unions as a group in order to prevent leapfrogging tactics. It also realised that Bevin was the union leader who really counted and who could be expected to lead the union side in a 'businesslike' manner [31] It was prepared to encourage union membership 'because it was only the unions who could enforce agreements whether on employees or recalcitrant employers'.[32]

A Whitley council was established in May 1919, and this provided negotiating and disputes machinery at three levels – national, district, and domestic. At national level the National Joint Industrial Council (NJIC) created a framework for the industry. As will be described below, this was comprehensive and effective. However, though the scope was broad, at an early stage the Federation decided that it would not discuss 'production or commercial matters' with the unions.[33] These it considered to be the subjects of managerial prerogatives. At district level, the Joint District Councils (JDCs) were to administer national agreements and to establish and maintain local agreements within the national framework. Joint Works Councils (JWCs) were to be primarily consultative and were not to reach agreements inconsistent with JDCs or the NJIC. The employers were least keen on the JWCs. Some felt that they were not much use in a highly centralised industrial relations system. Others felt that they were a means whereby union officials could gain access to the mills and that they were a potential threat to managerial prerogatives.[34] This reflected the Federation's policy of attempting to externalise or neutralise the union from the workplace. At an early date, for example, the Federation instructed its members not to communicate directly with union officials but always to go through the the Federation and its Local Associations.[35]

As well as creating a wage system which will be described in the next section, the NJIC also provided a disputes procedure. This had the usual interlocking stages and placed on both sides an obligation to keep the peace until a dispute had been through all the stages up to national level. On the whole the employers felt it was useful:[36] it could be used to resolve disputes; it allowed the employers to mobilise their collective strength around an issue; and under it the unions could be held responsible for disciplining their members and bringing other unions into line. The Federation saw the disputes machinery as a way of regulating the industry and building up a body of 'common law'.[37] Overall the employers valued the procedural machinery and were keen to preserve it.[38] However the main benefits of the national industrial relations system were in the area of wages and conditions.

II

Before 1918 wage bargaining in the industry was intermittent and re-stricted to certain localities and some of the larger mills.[39] Wartime arbi-tration awards brought about greater uniformity in wages and conditions, and during the war a number of district agreements were reached.[40] In December 1918 the Arbitration Court declined to deal with hours and overtime claims in the industry, since by then government policy was to leave such matters to be settled by the industry. This coincided with the emerging view of the FMEF which felt it should develop its own voluntary arrangements. Even before the establishment of the NJIC, the Feder-ation took the initiative and in February 1919 entered into an agreement with the unions on hours, overtime, and shift working. Looking back on the agreement the Federation's secretary saw it as a turning-point in the industry's industrial relations: 'Previously no miller knew what hours were being worked at a neighbouring mill . . . For the first time uniformity was established, and the first step was taken in that process of removing competition in labour from other forms of competition'.[41]

Between this agreement and the first wages agreement in the industry in July 1919, the unions continued to put in district and mill claims. Fearful of an upward spiralling of wages, the Federation instructed its members not to make concessions and produced its own wage structure plan. This was adopted and lasted, with only a few changes, throughout the interwar years and well into the post-Second World War period. The Federation realised that it would be impossible to enforce a single standard wage rate throughout the industry because of the diversity between large and small mills and different parts of the country. It therefore established a wage system based on the following principles: the country was divided up into five *classes*, ranging from the principal ports to rural villages; within each class, mills were then placed in three *grades* according to capacity; for each of these classes and grades a national *rate* was then fixed for the skilled rollerman at the top and the general labourer at the bottom of the scale. The rates of intermediate groups of mill workers were then settled by the JDCs, but subject to the guidelines and approval of the NJIC. In all it took three years to work out the detailed grading of mills and classification of areas. A large number of disputes and appeals were heard (employers looking for downgrading and the unions for upgrading) and a special Appeals Court, chaired by a KC, was established to hear contentious cases.[42]

The rates which were established were intended to be *maxima* and, for the most part, this appears to have been the case.[43] Such a tight system was possible because the industry was compact, relatively homogeneous in terms of technology and product, and used very little piecework. Though the industry was subject to competition, this was within the domestic market and therefore more amenable to control. Millers saw that they could use the national agreements to reduce competitive uncertainty and thereby stabilise their industry. Later when competition was brought under control by the MMA the national industrial relations system was used to lend support to this system. However, there was some payment over the rate, in the form of simple 'plusages' or the upgrading of jobs, especially for labourers. There was also some undercutting by small firms and non-federated firms; however this was not felt to be too serious.[44] Earnings quite closely followed rates and only started to deviate in the late 1930s when full employment and increased trade union power at workplace level began to push up earnings.[45]

The system, like multi-employer bargaining in other industries, was intended to prevent trade union leapfrogging; it was felt that by means of national negotiations 'competition between unions as to which can get the best out of the employers has been eliminated'.[46] Local bargaining it was felt 'would result in a constant state of unrest and ultimately the average wage would be unduly raised'.[47] The system of classification was also intended to reflect differences in the cost of living between areas. However, above all the aim was to reduce competition between firms and equalise wage costs. If local bargaining existed it was felt that 'to the existing competition in commercial matters would be added a competition in wages'.[48] As was pointed out, 'as between miller and miller, the Federation has established equitable difference in regard to the wages cost of manufacturing flour'.[49] Thus the system was intended to deal with competitive pressures in the industry and take wage costs out of competition.

Wages policy was thus used to further commercial policy. The employers knew that the industry suffered from excess capacity and that, because the demand for the product was inelastic, price competition meant a decline in the total revenue of the industry. Their object therefore was to regulate output and to reduce the competitive uncertainty in any way possible. More important, before the establishment of the

MMA, the employers saw their wage policy as a way of taking one element out of competition and thereby not aggravating commercial uncertainties. As a director of Ranks stated, as a result of 'the system of classification and grading, there is no competition in wages as between firm and firm and . . . there is an equitable difference between the wages of the large port mills, the inland mills, and the country mills. This has been a distinct advantage as it has probably meant the removal of a further factor that would have tended to increase competition'.[50] After the establishment of the MMA the employers saw the wage system as a means of enforcing their product market and price arrangements. Their object was not to equalise wages, but to equalise wage costs. By grading mills according to their capacity, they were in effect grading them according to their production costs and were attempting to establish competitive equality between firms. An FMEF survey of the wage costs of flour production considered that this had been achieved: 'by classification and differentiation of wages the Federation has done everything to make the conditions in the industry as between miller and miller fair, as the cost of manufacture has been practically equalised'.[51]

This system brought considerable stability to wages in flour milling throughout the interwar years. There were no changes in wage rates between 1924 and 1939, and as a result relative earnings fell from the mid-1930s onwards.

The flour milling industry also introduced a number of innovative terms and conditions of employment, all of a progressive nature, but some of which also helped reduce the competitive uncertainty of the industry. Thus, in February 1919, the employers conceded a week's paid holiday, long before most other industries. A later agreement of April 1920 (in the industry referred to as the guaranteed week and security agreement) introduced joint consultation at mill level to regulate short-time working and avoid lay-offs. Where this was not possible, the agreement laid down that employers were to give one week's notice or payment in lieu. Thus, though the agreement did not guarantee continuous employment, it did prevent employers laying their workers off for one or two days a week and ensured them a week's work or a week's pay. However this had the unintended consequence of reducing the incentive to operate short-time. As a result in the mid-1920s the employers contemplated an industry-wide supplementary unemployment benefit scheme to subsidise short-time working collectively. In part because of legal difficulties this was not introduced. An agreement in 1937 guaranteed workers the same amount of money when on short-time as when fully employed. Again this was an incentive to run mills full-time. The idea of a supplementary unemployment benefit scheme was therefore resurrected, with the aim that firms should share the cost of short-time work and thereby reduce the tendency to overproduction. Again there were legal problems and nothing came of the proposed scheme, but the 1937 agreement did provide greater continuity of employment.[52]

Another area where the industry was innovative was in the field of redundancy payments. The establishment of the MMA in 1929, entailing as it did the buying up and destruction of capacity, quickly raised the prospect of redundancy. In return for union support with rationalisation, Bevin suggested that the industry should introduce a scheme to deal with redundancy.[53] In 1929 a scheme was established whereby funds were made available to the NJIC from the MMA and also from individual firms involved in rationalisation. This fund was jointly administered – though the Federation throughout insisted that the scheme in no way undermined management's right to reorganise their mills or make workers redundant.[54] Relief was paid out to supplement unemployment benefit, but the main aim was the resettlement of redundant workers. Older men were paid retirement annuities; younger men were helped transfer to other jobs (if possible in the industry – a Register of Unemployed Workers being established in 1930 to facilitate this); and some were given lump sums to help set up in small business. Though the sums were not large and though only about 2,000 men were involved, Bevin for one thought the scheme was of great value.[55] In part the scheme may have been motivated by genuine humanitarian concerns and a desire to supplement state unemployment benefit.[56] However, there was also a shrewd understanding on the part of the employers that rationalisation would proceed more smoothly with union support.[57]

From its early days the Federation had considered a pension scheme for the industry. After considerable planning in 1931 an industry-wide contributory scheme, jointly administered with the unions, came into existence. Membership was compulsory for all new employees. The aim was to attract and retain good young workers (the scheme was transferable between firms within the industry) and to encourage older workers to retire.[58] In many respects the scheme (though neither large nor generous) was unique in that it was industry-wide, jointly-administered, and transferable within the industry.

The initiative for these schemes came mainly from the employers. The origins in part reflected a traditional paternalism. However they also indicated a shrewd and enlightened self-interest.

III

This system survived into the post-Second World War period. The story of its demise in the 1960s and 1970s cannot be told in any great detail. However a few general points may be here. It was not undermined by a challenge from workplace bargaining, in the manner described by the Donovan Commission, as labour militancy and shopfloor bargaining were never very strong in the industry. Nor was it much affected by the promptings of government for industrial relations reform. Change came about more because of significant economic, structural, and technological transformations in the post-Second World War period which had a profound effect on its industrial relations system.

After decontrol in 1953 demand fell as, with rising living standards, consumers continued to switch to other foodstuffs.[59] The Monopolies and Restrictive Trade Practices Act of 1948 and the later Restrictive Trade Practices Act of 1956 and the Resale Price Act of 1964 led to the progressive dismantling of the industry's market-sharing and price-fixing arrangements.[60] In this situation of unfavourable demand and renewed competition, the large firms in the industry pursued new strategies: there were further acquisitions in the 1960s leading to a consolidation of the dominant position of the Rank Hovis McDougall and Spillers; both these firms then integrated forward into baking; at the same time the large baking group, Associated British Foods, integrated backwards into flour milling to secure its source of supply; and all three groups diversified more widely into other foodstuffs. At the same time the industry witnessed important technological changes with the introduction of faster milling machines, electrical and electronic control, and more sophisticated pneumatic conveyancing and improved bulk transportation systems.

At first, during and immediately after the war, the industry's national industrial relations system continued to develop. It became more comprehensive in coverage as the National Arbitration Tribunal ordered nonfederated firms to observe the national wages agreement.[61] New wage agreements were negotiated for women, youths, and transport workers. The national wage system remained tight, with rates being considered to be both minima and maxima well into the late 1950s.[62] However, though this still had some advantages, in a changing market and technological situation it also had growing disadvantages.

Through the 1950s, the national system failed to adapt to changing circumstances and increasingly failed to perform its initial regulatory function. Changes could not be made sufficiently frequently in the national and district rates to allow for changing circumstances and wage increases in other industries. Voices started to be heard that the wage system was too inflexible: the unions began to complain about the complicated classification and grade system and to think in terms of plant bargaining; likewise some employers began to see the value of relating wages more closely to their company and mill circumstances.[63] Above all in a situation of increased competition, firms felt the need to negotiate about wages and working practices at company and mill level so as to obtain a better utilisation of machinery and manpower and reduce their operating costs. As an industry spokesman said, 'When price agreements had to be abandoned, other collective arrangements needed also to be reframed'.[64]

In 1950 the system of grading was abolished. In 1958 the elaborate classification system was reduced from five to three and later in 1962 to two classes. The main change, however, came in 1965 when, prompted by Rank Hovis McDougall, the NJIC negotiated a so-called 'flexibility clause' in the national agreement which allowed for company and mill bargaining on wage rates geared to local productivity. Under this clause the leading firms introduced job evaluated wage structures, reduced manning levels, and instituted more flexible systems of continuous working based on three- and four-shift arrangements. This allowed them to gain full benefit from the new machinery as mills were remodelled.[65] In these circumstances the national agreement became less and less important, so that by the mid-1970s it had become a loose safety-net agreement fixing a single minimum rate and basic hours. As such it is relatively unimportant to the main firms in the industry. From the mid-1960s onwards, the large diversified companies (for whom flour milling was now only a small part of their activities) set about creating internal industrial relations systems. They developed their managerial hierarchies and their own personnel capabilities.[66] These were based on their different divisions, though certain conditions such as pensions were common throughout each company.

Some of the other terms and conditions, which had been a great pride of the industry in the inter-war years, also failed to adapt to changing circumstances. The pension scheme failed to adjust its contributions and benefits and was slowly superseded by improved state benefits and even more so by companies' own schemes. In the early 1970s both Rank Hovis McDougall and Spillers withdrew and in 1978 it was wound up.[67] The security agreement also continued, but was less necessary in the full-employment post-war period.[68] Significantly, individual firms introduced sick-pay schemes before the NJIC which only agreed a scheme in 1962 and one moreover which was less favourable than that in most individual firms. It is also revealing that, when mill closures accelerated in the late 1950s and early 1960s, the Federation decided that redundancy arrangements were the responsibility of individual firms.[69] The national disputes procedure still survives, but is little used, and the main firms prefer that cases do not go beyond company level.

IV

It is hoped that this case study provides some insights into the relationship between employers' commercial policies and their labour market strategies. In the inter-war years, the desire to regulate competition and to support collusive product market arrangements were important factors behind the development of industry-wide collective bargaining in the flour milling industry. The comprehensive nature of the wage system which developed was also facilitated by the compact and homogeneous nature of that industry. However, without collusion in the one area, employer solidarity in the other area would have been less effective. In the post-Second World War period, the breakdown of restrictive practices and the growth of competition were important factors driving firms to develop new industrial relations policies based on mill- and company-level bargaining. By the 1960s, the large and increasingly diversified firms in the industry had less incentive to cooperate and more desire to achieve a competitive advantage in whatever way possible. They also had a greater capability to develop their own internal systems to coordinate their more complex activities.

The case of flour milling may be a somewhat extreme example of the tightness of a national agreement in the inter-war years and its demise in the post-war period. However product market factors also affected industrial relations systems in other industries. This perspective suggests a different interpretation of the rise and fall of national bargaining in British industry and shifts the explanation away from a predominant emphasis on factors endogenous to industrial relations and more towards the product market and commercial position of the employer.

University of Kent at Canterbury
and
Business History Unit,
London School of Economics

NOTES

1. A. Smith, *The Wealth of Nations*, E. Cannan (ed.), (London, 1950), Vol.1, Book 1, Ch.7, p.63.
2. Ibid., p.68.
3. There are constant statements to this effect in the record of the industry's National Joint Industrial Council, but see in particular *NJIC Annual Report 1943–44* and Japanese visit *NJIC Annual Report 1950–51*. Sir H. Betterton, Minister of Labour, *Ministry of Labour Gazette*, March 1922. p.83. See also L.H. Green, 'Labour Problems in the British Flour Milling Industry: An Experiment in the Ordering of Industrial Relations', in F.E. Gannett and B.F. Catherwood, *Industrial and Labour Relations in Great Britain* (London, 1939). For a favourable assessment by a historian see R. Charles, *The Development of Industrial Relations in Britain 1911-1939* (London, 1973), pp.165–7.
4. Royal Commission on Trade Unions and Employers' Association, *Report*, Cmnd. 3623, (1968); H.A. Clegg, *The System of Industrial Relations in Great Britain*, (Oxford, 1970), chapters 1,6 and 7.
5. G.C. Allen, *Monopoly and Restrictive Practices* (London, 1968); D.C. Coleman, 'Combinations of Capital and Labour in the English Paper Industry, 1789-1825' *Economica*, Vol.XXI, No.1, Feb. 1954; H.W. McCrosty, *The Trust Movement in Britain* (London, 1906); A.H. Hunter, *Competition and the Law* (London, 1966).
6. J.M. Rees, *Trusts in British Industry 1914-1921* (London, 1922), p.27.
7. Committee on Trusts, *Report* Cd. 9236 (1918) p.2; J. Hilton, *A Study of Trade Organisations and Combinations in the UK* (1919); G.C. Allen, op. cit., Ch.4.
8. H.A. Marquand, *Dynamics of Industrial Combination* (London, 1931); A.F. Lucas, *Industrial Reconstruction and the Control of Competition (London, 1937)*.
9. Committee on Industry and Trade, *Final Report* (1929), pp.176–7; see also Board of Trade, *Restraint of Trade* (1931), pp.6–7.
10. L. Hannah, *The Rise of the Corporate Economy* (London, 1976), p.136; 'The Cartelisation of England', *The Economist* (18 March 1939).
11. A.E. Humphries, 'Wartime Control of Breadstuffs', *The Miller*, 22 April 1935, p.379; *Milling*, 2 Aug. 1963; *Milling*, 3 Aug. 1966.
12. A.H. Hurst, *The Bread of Britain* (London, 1930), p.28; *The Record*, January 1933, p.189.
13. H. McCrosty, 'The Grainmilling Industry: A Study in Organisation'. *Economic Journal*, Vol.XIII (1903). p.324.
14. Ibid.

15. H.V. Edwards, 'Flour Milling', in M.P. Fogarty (ed.), *Further Studies in Industrial Organisation* (London, 1948).
16. The activities of the MMA were kept secret. The following account is drawn from H.V. Edwards, op. cit.; A.F. Lucas, *Industrial Reconstruction and the Control of Competition*, (London, 1937); R. Desbrow, 'History of the Structure of the British Flour Milling Industry', *The Miller*, 3 April 1950.
17. H.V. Edwards, op. cit., p.65; G.D.N. Worswick and D.G. Tipping, *Profits in the British Economy 1909–1938* (Oxford, 1967), p.99.
18. Flour Milling Employers' Federation (FMEF), Minute Book Volume VI, Points concerning Labour Position in the Flour Milling Industry, 31 March 1933.
19. FMEF, VI, Point Concerning Labour Position in the Industry, 31 March 1933; see also National Board for Prices and Incomes, Report No.3, *Prices of Bread and Flour*, Cmnd. 2760 (London, 1965), p.4.
20. H.V. Edwards, op. cit., p.29.
21. Even in the big firms paternalism persisted from rural and small town origins. See, for example, J. Rank Ltd., *The Master Millers: The Story of the House of Rank* (London, 1955), p.56.
22. L.H. Green, 'Labour Problems in the Flour Milling Industry', *The Miller*, 22 April 1935, p.399; E. Bevin, 'The National Joint Industrial Council', *Milling*, 13 April 1935.
23. *The Bulletin of the Flour Milling Employers' Federation*, 1921, p.2. In 1919 there were nine unions on the Flour Milling NJIC; by 1929 this had been reduced to the Transport and General Workers Union, the National Union of General and Municipal Workers, and the National Union of Distributive and Allied Workers which organised in CWS mills.
24. *The Miller*, 22 April 1935, p.399
25. *The Miller*, 3 June 1918, 2 Sept. 1918, 22 April 1933.
26. The Committee on Relations between Employers and Employed, a Sub-Committee of the Cabinet Committee on Reconstruction, under the Chairmanship of Mr J.H. Whitley, recommended the establishment of Joint Industrial Councils in those industries where collective bargaining did not exist. See Ministry of Reconstruction, *Interim Report of Committee on Relations between Employers and Employed*, Cd.8606, (1917–18).
27. FMEF, III, Management Board, 11 Nov. 1920.
28. H.V. Edwards, op. cit. p.49. This figure excludes CWS and Scottish CWS output, both of which were outside the Federation, but co-operated closely with it.
29. See H.F. Gospel, 'Employers' Organisations: Their Growth and Function in the British System of Industrial Relations 1918–1939' (London Ph.D., 1974), pp.101-6. FMEF, II, Labour Advisory Committee, 8 Nov. 1918.
30. FMEF, III, Investigation Committee, 16 Sept. 1926.
31. FMEF, III, Investigation Committee, 16 Sept. 1926.
32. FMEF, V, Board, 9 June 1926.
33. FMEF, II, Provisional Board, 11 Dec. 1918.
34. FMEF, V, Board, 9 June 1926.
35. FMEF, II, Executive Committee, 23 April 1919.
36. See H.F. Gospel, op. cit., pp.164–93.
37. FMEF, V, Investigation Committee, *Report*, paras 10-11 12 Jan. 1927.
38. See the discussions on the Investigation Committee set up after the General Strike. FMEF, III.
39. *Milling*, 1 March 1963, refers to a local Hull agreement in 1890.
40. *The Miller*, 6 May 1918, p.115, and 2 Sept. 1918, p.346.
41. L.H. Green, 'Labour Problems in the Flour Milling Industry', *The Miller*, 22 April 1935, p.400.
42. *NJIC Annual Report 1920–21*, pp.9-10.
43. See H.F. Gospel, op. cit. pp.228–9 and 273–6.
44. Ibid., pp.274-5.
45. Ibid., pp.275-6.
46. FMEF, V, Board, 9 June 1926.

47. FMEF, III, Special Negotiating Committee, 2 March 1921. The system brought considerable stability to wages in flour milling throughout the inter-war years. There were no changes in wage rates between 1924 and 1939.
48. FMEF, V, Investigation Committee *Report*, para 22, 12 Jan. 1927.
49. FMEF, I, NJIC Employers' Executive Committee, 23 Feb. 1922.
50. W.H. Raylor, FMEF. V, Board, 17 April 1927.
51. FMEF, I, Management Committee, 29 Sept. 1921; see also FMEF, VII, Board, 11 May 1922.
52. See H.F. Gospel, op. cit., pp.247-51 for full details of these various schemes and plans. For a positive union comment see the view expressed by T. Healy of the TGWU in *Milling*, Jan. 1970.
53. FMEF, VI, Executive Committee, 14 Nov. 1929.
54. FMEF, VI, Executive Committee, 31 Jan. 1930.
55. E. Bevin, *Milling*, 13 April 1935, p.423; FMEF, VII, Board, 11 May 1932; for more detail see H.F. Gospel, op. cit., pp.251-4.
56. FMEF, VI, Executive Committee, 14 Nov. 1929.
57. FMEF, VI, MMA and NJIC Meeting, 14 Nov. 1929.
58. FMEF, VI, Executive Committee, 10 April 1929.
59. For a useful analysis see *Milling*, 9 Sept. 1966; *Milling*, 6 Jan. 1967; *Milling*, 16 June 1967.
60. For general background see G.C. Allen, op. cit. (London, 1968), pp.55-8 and Political and Economic Planning, *Industrial Trade Associations* (London, 1957), Ch.10. For more detail see Registrar of Restrictive Trading Agreements, *Report 7 August 1956 to 31 December 1959*, Cmnd. 1273 (1959), p.30. For some of the views of the flour milling industry see *Milling*, 14 Oct. 1960; *Milling*, 13 Jan. 1967.
61. *NJIC Annual Report 1940–41*.
62. *NJIC Annual Report 1957-58*.
63. *Milling*, 9 March 1962; *NJIC Annual Report 1949–50*; *NJIC Annual Report 1957–58*.
64. *Milling*, 13 Jan. 1967.
65. *Milling*, 10 June 1966; *Milling*, 17 June 1966; *Milling*, 29 Sept. 1967; *NJIC Annual Report 1964–65*;
66. Interview with D.C.R. Scott, ex-Chief Executive Personnel, Rank Hovis McDougall, 11 July 1983. Interview with A. Knight, Personnel Manager, British Bakeries, Rank Hovis McDougall, 7 Dec. 1983.
67. *NJIC Annual Report 1972–73*.
68. *NJIC Annual Report 1947-48*.
69. *NJIC Annual Report 1957–58* and *NJIC Annual Report 1959–60*.

TRADE UNIONS, MANAGEMENT AND THE SEARCH FOR PRODUCTION IN THE COVENTRY MOTOR CAR INDUSTRY, 1939–75

By TOM DONNELLY and DAVID THOMS

I. Introduction

This essay examines the interaction between management and the trade unions in the assembly branch of the motor car industry in Coventry from 1939 until the mid-1970s. Attention is focused upon the production strategies adopted by management towards organised labour as a result of external stimuli, and the responses which these drew from the trade unions. At the beginning of the war organised labour was still in its infancy within the motor industry with union penetration in Coventry largely restricted to the toolrooms and craft shops. The accelerated development of the city's industrial base during the Second World War created the opportunity for significant growth in the bargaining position of the trade unions, an important change in the balance of industrial power between management and labour which was consolidated further in the expansionary climate of the post-war decades. The motor industry became synonymous with large, well organised trade unions, particularly the Transport and General Worker's Union and the Amalgamated Engineering Union, which imposed a measure of external constraint upon management unknown before 1939. The drive for production throughout the war years and beyond brought an uneasy accommodation between management and labour during which control of the shop floor was largely ceded to the unions, a strategy which eventually proved untenable in the more competitive climate of the 1970s.

Although by 1939 Coventry had lost its earlier, dominant, role in motor car manufacture, it remained an important centre for the assembly of both specialist and popular vehicles.[1] At the start of the 1930s the Singer Motor Co. was Coventry's leading volume producer, but its subsequent demise meant that by the end of the decade Rootes and Standard were the city's only representatives among 'The Big Six'. Over 30 other Coventry firms claimed to manufacture cars and, while most of these were extremely modest operations, several were among the country's leading producers of luxury and sports vehicles, including Daimler, Alvis and Jaguar. Although output was concentrated among relatively large firms, decision-making was often controlled by a small number of individuals, some of whom were closely associated with the creation or early development of their firms. By 1968, when the British Leyland Motor Co. was formed, Coventry's two volume manufacturers were together responsible for about 18.0 per cent of car output in Britain compared with around 20 per cent for their respective predecessor companies in 1939.[2] However, these figures create a false impression of continuity, for the intervening period was a time of mergers and take-overs which saw Standard joining forces with Leyland, the Lancashire bus and truck company (1961), and Rootes finally relinquishing control to the Chrysler Corporation of America (1967). By 1968 Jaguar was the sole survivor of Coventry's specialist car companies, albeit as part of British Motor Holdings (1966). With the exception of William Lyons at Jaguar, the leading motor entrepreneurs of the 1930s were no longer active in the motor industry, while management structures and methods had also changed significantly since the pre-war years. The formation of BLMC in 1968 was not only a watershed for car assembly in Coventry but for the British motor vehicle industry as a whole. It signalled the beginning of a period which has become associated with the financial crises of the mid-1970s. This culminated in the government rescue of both Chrysler and BL, and interventions which in turn contributed to the establishment of a new relationship between management and trade unions.

II. The Impact of War

Many of Coventry's leading motor vehicle companies were brought into the rearmament drive of the late 1930s. Diversification increased rapidly after September 1939 with the industry becoming associated in particular with production of aero engines and other aircraft components, and armoured vehicles. Standard, Daimler and Rootes were all closely involved in the aero engine shadow scheme while at the same time manufacturing a wide range of other products from scout cars and ambulances to fire pumps and bomb release clips. Management of the newly constructed shadow factories was placed with the motor vehicles firms in the belief that the mass production methods pioneered by the industry could be applied to the manufacture of aircraft and, although this proved difficult to achieve, they did contribute substantially to the overall growth in aero engine output.[3] The motor companies also acted as sub-contractors to other firms. Alvis and Rover, for example, both did work for Rolls Royce, while Standard had contracts for the manufacture of Beaufighter fuselages, De Havilland Mosquito and Oxford trainer aircraft.[4] These developments significantly inflated the level of productive activity for which the motor vehicle companies were responsible. New factories were built, plant installed and labour recruited, while under conditions of near monopsony government departments demanded a swift response to rapidly changing output targets and product specifications. Inevitably, the relationship between management and the trade unions entered a new phase, some of the results of which were to have long-term repercussions.

The conduct of industrial relations was influenced in particular by the labour shortages which characterised Coventry's engineering sector from about 1936. By the outbreak of war the local market for skilled engineering workers was acutely competitive, with members of the Coventry and District Engineering Employers' Association (CDEEA) breaking their own rules by offering inducements in order to attract suitable recruits. A high level of labour turnover continued into the summer of 1940 until government restrictions began to take effect. An increase in the local employment participation ratio, together with the recruitment of migrant workers, helped to ease the situation, though the industrial Midlands remained an area of serious labour shortage, particularly in engineering, until 1944 after which the impact of lend-lease and the changing circumstances of the war began to be felt.

Shortages of trained labour led to de-skilling and, although dilution in the engineering industry in general progressed fairly slowly at the beginning of the war, it was accelerated by the implementation in 1940 of the national agreement between the Amalgamated Engineering Union and the engineering employers which allowed for much greater flexibility in the operation of machine shops. It seems likely too that dilution occurred relatively quickly in Coventry where payment of the skilled rate was linked to the nature of the job rather than length or degree of training.[5] Dilution came to include the large scale recruitment of female labour to the shop floor, and sometimes even the toolrooms, which had formerly been the preserve of male workers. Yet many firms experienced considerable difficulty in recruiting female labour, particularly married women, so that this was only a partial solution to the labour supply problem. Changes in the organisation and hours of work were introduced in order to accelerate throughput. Relatively little use was made of formal work study techniques, but the reorganisation of shop floor layout was often successfully applied to the reduction of output blockages. With the onset of war several Coventry firms increased working hours by 20 per cent or more, pushing well beyond the regulatory norms for the engineering industry. Despite a growth in absenteeism and the recognition that long working hours could reduce efficiency, this remained a key aspect of the production strategy of management until the later stages of the war.

These initiatives required the support of the workforce and its trade union representatives. The war helped to strengthen labour organisation in the motor industry which before 1939 was in its infancy in Coventry as elsewhere.[6] The concessions granted from 1940 by the larger Coventry employers were not always simply a passive acceptance of the inevitable but rather a reflection of management realism and a desire to benefit from collective bargaining and conciliation. One senior government official described Coventry's motor industry as 'modern, aggressive, "hard boiled" in its outlook – very well organised but rather inhuman in its relations with labour'.[7] This comment suggests that management was no pushover and that the relative ease with which the official trade union structure developed was in part a calculated attempt by the employers to serve their own interests. Local trade union officials were generally supportive of the employers' attempts to meet output targets, while the often lengthy conciliation procedures could help to deflate a potentially damaging industrial conflict. The greatest threat to the autonomy of management frequently arose from the shop floor and under these circumstances the relative conservatism of many local union officials may have been welcomed by management as a valuable antidote to this type of radicalism.

In the early months of war many employers, including the powerful Standard Motor Company, attempted to resist the growth of organised labour, but the need to satisfy government orders soon encouraged a more pragmatic attitude. There was, however, prolonged resistance to the creation of even informal machinery for the discussion of issues concerned with works' organisation. Joint Production Committees were gradually introduced in Coventry in 1942 but only after pressure was applied by the Midland Regional Board and there is no evidence to suggest that they developed a significant managerial function. Management succeeded in restricting the role of organised labour to highly specific shop floor issues.

Attempts were made to alleviate the problems associated with long working hours through adjustments to the physical environment and general conditions of employment but financial inducements continued to be the principal method of securing labour cooperation. Coventry soon acquired a reputation for exceptionally high wage levels in the engineering industry, even within the generally prosperous West Midlands. The cost plus system which the government used to price contracts at the beginning of the war did not encourage efficiency but even when this was changed labour scarcity and rapid alterations in the nature of the job placed considerable pressure upon piece rates. The Coventry Tool Room Agreement of 1941, which was designed to protect the incomes of apprentice-trained craftsmen, also proved wage inflationary since toolmakers' earnings, which drifted upwards, were used as a negotiating guide by other groups of workers. By 1943 the government was so alarmed that an official investigation was set up to examine the level of earnings in the city's aircraft industry. Its report noted that 'The basis of the problem appeared to be the fixing of times and prices which result in high earnings without a corresponding high effort'.[8] The demotivating effects of high wage levels were known to Coventry's employers but in the circumstances of the period, and with piece rate manipulation firmly established as a management tool, they were unable to keep rates down.

The trade union response to the onset of war and the growth of the engineering labour force was to strengthen its own membership and organisation. Competition for members and the need to show results rendered some officials particularly demanding in their approach to management but this attitude appears to have moderated as the situation stabilised and the unions set about consolidating their own position. An important feature of this consolidation was the affirmation of union authority over shop floor dissidents. The expansion of the shop stewards movement was an important aspect of the development of organised labour in Coventry during this period, though by 1941 only Daimler and Standard among the car firms actually allowed stewards time off during working hours to conduct their union affairs. Inevitably the stewards posed a threat to the authority of local officials but perhaps a more difficult problem involved groups of dissident workers whose chief concern was for immediate improvements in conditions of work, especially pay, regardless of external constraints. To some extent, therefore, union officials were propelled into a negotiating position which was not always of their own choice. Writing of Coventry, the Ministry of Labour's local conciliation officer noted in March 1941 that 'It would be true to say that responsible Trade Union Officials offer no support to the initiation of claims for unreasonable wage levels, but they are frequently placed in an embarrassing position by pressure from elements operating within the workshops, and have no alternative other than to pursue the claims of their members'.[9]

Disputes arose over a number of issues, from alleged breaches of agreements by employers to victimization of shop floor workers. Yet, with the exception of Rootes' Humber-Hillman works, Coventry's wartime strike record appears to have been relatively good. For example, between January 1943 and December 1944 the aircraft industry as a whole suffered 182 major strikes, but of the most serious involving the loss of at least 10,000 man hours only one (Rootes) was located in Coventry.[10] Local union officials were generally assiduous in avoiding loss of production, often taking a decisive lead in defusing unofficial action and persuading employees to return to work. Significantly, the Ministry of Labour's local representatives commented favourably upon the conduct of labour relations among those firms in the Midlands which were unionised compared with those which were not. Apart from the commitment to the war effort of men such as Jack Jones, the local conciliation machinery helped to reduce the temperature of industrial disputes.[11] Although the works conferences involving the Engineering Employers' Association and the unions frequently ended in a 'failure to agree', views were aired and the opportunity taken to consider rationally the wider significance of strike action.

The wartime conduct of industrial relations contained important implications for the development of Coventry's motor vehicle industry after 1945. The co-operation of the war years helped to ensure an orderly adjustment to the changing employment conditions of 1944 and 1945. In the longer term, however, the tradition of hight wage rates together with the evolution of the Gang system created a number of problems with which management found it difficult to grapple. By 1945 the balance of power between management and labour had shifted dramatically since the start of the war. The catalyst of this change was the war itself but it was particularly significant that the bulk of Coventry's motor vehicle industry became linked with the growth sector of aircraft where the imperative to meet government orders took precedence over almost everything else. Moreover, while the trade unions became organised, individually and as a group, management continued to operate independently and in the process undermined the collective strength of its own organisation.

III. The Gang System

By the spring of 1944 management and labour were both beginning to prepare for a return to post-war conditions, an exercise which generated considerable uncertainty within the motor industry as a whole. Many Coventry manufacturers were unsure of their ability to convert their premises to peacetime production whilst maintaining high levels of output and pay during a period when the market was expected to be highly competitive once government orders began to contract. Similarly, labour had no wish to revert to the seasonal nature of employment and the often harsh conditions endured before 1939, and was also anxious to keep the substantially improved levels of earnings the war had brought. With these issues in mind, John Black, managing director of Standard since 1934, informed Hugh Dalton, with whom he was on close personal terms, that a return to normal vehicle production could only be achieved if the government could ensure a steady supply of steel, light alloys, forgings and castings. Black emphasised that the motor industry would be a vital element in Britain's reconstruction and that the authorities should do everything in their power to assist progress once peace had returned, including the prevention of labour dislocation. Dalton readily agreed with this and, though trade union officials did not dissent, their main concern was to secure continuation of the generally advantageous relationship which they enjoyed with management during the war period. Their unease was justified since by the beginning of 1945 there were already indications of a return to a more authoritarian style of management in Coventry with attempts to deflate wages and talk of redundancy. Many workers viewed the closure of the Nuffield Mechanisation plant that year as a portent of things to come. Soon after the war ended, and just when stop stewards were demanding that existing wage levels be maintained, the management announced that the Nuffield works was no longer central to the Morris operation and simply closed it without any form of consultation.[12]

Trade union anxieties over redundancies and a possible return to the labour relations of the previous decade were crystallised by events at Rootes' Humber plant where the works manager had for some months adopted an unusually abrasive attitude towards the work force. Complaints made against him at a Works Conference ranged from an alleged refusal to permit payments of a subsistence allowance to padlocking the tea urns. The firm's labour relations eventually deteriorated so badly that, despite the intervention of union officials, nearly 5,000 men came out on unofficial strike for nine days. When work did resume the atmosphere within the plant was more of a truce than industrial peace. Mistrust and friction on both sides continued into the following year when the firm tried to enforce a wage cut at the old Humber factory which had long suffered a reputation for low productivity, poor pay and a high level of discontent. The immediate cause of the trouble was an attempt to break locally agreed wage rates, coupled with the installation of new and more efficient machinery which, it was feared, would lead to redundancy. The workers responded by adopting a go-slow which reduced output to one vehicle per week. Retaliation was swift and involved the dismissal of 500 men. This precipitated an acrimonious strike lasting four weeks before a settlement was reached in which only 50 per cent of those sacked were reinstated. Rootes had come under pressure from other firms to put its house in order as no one wanted such disputes to spread to other factories and there is little doubt that this external pressure was a potent factor in resolving what had become a dangerous situation. These and similar events during 1945–46 demonstrated that there could be no return to the style of labour relations which had existed from the 1922 lock-out down to the Second World War.[13] It was widely recognised that co-operation between both sides of the motor industry was essential if an orderly return to peacetime production and industrial prosperity was to be achieved. It was this imperative that helped to give Coventry its distinctive style of labour relations from the late 1940s until the mid-1970s.[14]

The UK motor car industry prospered in the two decades after the war with production peaking at 1.8 million vehicles in 1964. Until the mid-1950s British exports did well in what was virtually a seller's market. Between 1948 and 1952 the proportion of output exported varied from 62 to 77 per cent after which it dropped to around 50 per cent. Coventry shared in this prosperity and in 1951 local output amounted to nearly 28 per cent of total UK production after which it began to fall fairly steadily so that by 1964 its contribution was only 19 per cent of the total. Over the following eight years national output fell and then stagnated before the 'Barber Boom' pushed it to a new record of 1.9 million units in 1972. Yet although Coventry benefited from this expansion it still only commanded some 20 per cent of the UK total. Thus long before the UK industry as a whole fell into the crisis of the mid-1970s the city was already in decline as a major centre of car production, and this framework should be borne in mind when examining labour relations in the Coventry sector of the industry.[15]

During the war the Gang system had become firmly entrenched in the main Coventry factories. The rigidity of the labour market allowed the Gangs and the shop stewards, who were invariably Gang leaders, to assume an important role in the running of the factories. Despite high levels of inward migration, labour shortages continued for more than a decade with unemployment in the city usually hovering below one per cent. As early as 1944 Black had tried to persuade his colleagues in the CDEEA of the need to evolve a coherent policy towards the work force, suggesting that it should receive a high, but fixed, wage rate. Although his ideas were rejected, Black made it clear that he intended to pursue his own policy regardless of the CDEEA which responded by expelling Standard from its ranks.[16] The suspicion remains, however, that Black may have deliberately engineered this episode in order to free his company from the general constraints imposed by the CDEEA. Indeed, it was the policy which he then adopted that came to represent the apogee of the Coventry Gang system.

The structure evolved by Black owed much to Standard's tradition of welfarism dating back to the First World War when the company introduced a benevolent fund, inaugurated child care arrangements for women workers and established canteen and recreational facilities. In 1936 Black took the initiative in founding the Standard Employees' Special Fund to provide sickness and death benefits, group life insurance, and pensions for those with at least fifteen years' service. The firm appears to have believed that such schemes encouraged loyalty among the work force, compensation perhaps for the tough management style which came to be associated with Standard during the 1930s. Black also recognised, however, that the trade unions had become a force to be reckoned with and that a positive approach to welfare questions would help to buy the co-operation that was essential if the company was to become a more dominant force among the 'Big Six'.[17]

Black's strategy was to formalise and institutionalise both unions and the Gangs and to convert piecework into a policy of Responsible Autonomy which would operate as an incentive towards the quadruple goal of high output, productivity, profits and wages. Piecework was therefore the driving force. In 1945 there was a plethora of Gangs in Standard's plants with bonus rates varying from 175 to 250 per cent above base rates. Black ended this, organising the Canley work force into 15 Gangs, a reduction from 104, and scaling down the number of grades of workers from 68 to 8. The working week was reduced from 44 to 42½ hours. A minimum bonus of 100 per cent was guaranteed compared with the CDEEA's minimum of 27.5 per cent, though in practice the latter figure was closer to 60 per cent. At the Banner Lane tractor plant, however, the workers were organised into one large Gang, though everyone was guaranteed a minimum weekly wage of £5. This was essentially a self-regulating system of shop floor management which devolved considerable power to the shop stewards. Under the principle of mutuality the shop stewards were responsible for negotiating the price of jobs and the distribution of workers between jobs, as well as manning levels and track speeds. Under this arrangement foremen and other supervisory staff were effectively marginalised within the management structure. In practice almost total control of the shop floor was ceded to the stewards and the payments mechanism was used to pace production with a close relationship existing between work effort, output and rewards. All labour was hired through the union office and it was the stewards who decided the amount of overtime to be worked. On average wages rose from 42 per cent above the industry average in 1947 to 78 per cent in 1950, though subsequently falling back to just over 60 per cent; in Coventry other firms, especially Rootes, began to close the earnings gap with Standard in the early 1950s. Finally, it has been argued that because of the quasi-managerial role played by the shop stewards, the company's administrative costs were between three and five per cent below those of comparable establishments.[18]

There is a danger in elevating the Gang system at Standard to the status of an ideal model and, as will be shown later, it did not change the firm's position within the 'Big Six'. For the moment, however, it is important to note that although Rootes and Jaguar, the other major car firms in the city, adopted variants of the Gang system, their versions differed in certain key respects from the Black model. Rootes only gave full recognition to trade unions in 1950 but then managerial prerogatives were ceded to the shop-floor as the stewards assumed responsibility for the booking in and out of work, the loading levels and pace of the track. The Ryton plant eventually came to be described as a 'self-governing republic'[19] with piecework being the surrogate foreman, driving the work force to greater effort. At Standard power was devolved downwards voluntarily by management but this does not appear to have been the case at Rootes. Although the firm's leadership appeared to take a strong position on managerial rights, in practice it was ready to concede over small issues in order to keep production going. There was little direct supervision in the shops and, as Tolliday has rightly concluded, this was 'management by abdication'.[20] The third variant was at Jaguar where after officially recognising unions in 1946, William Lyons spent the next five years trying to dislodge them, but failed mainly because of the strength of the National Union of Vehicle Builders, on the skills of whose members the company was so dependent for the production of its luxury products. As with Rootes and Standard, piecework earnings represented the main incentive to greater effort, though by contrast Gangs tended to be relatively small. This was because with the skilled labour required to make high quality cars and a stable model range and strong market position there was little need for the near continuous process of shop-floor bargaining that characterised the volume producers. At Jaguar management decided on loading and manning levels so that very little power was devolved to the shop-floor.

The heyday of the Gang system, especially the Standard variety, was short-lived. It functioned well in the late 1940s, partly because of Black's quixotic style of management but also because it was in the unions' interest for it to succeed. In addition, the buoyant market meant that cost control became of secondary importance to the drive for production. By the mid-1950s, when markets became more competitive, both Rootes and Standard found it increasingly difficult to survive the challenge from BMC, Ford and at times even Vauxhall. Neither firm enjoyed any significant economies of scale so that both found it extremely difficult to retain their share of the volume market. Apart from early rounds of capital investment in the immediate post-war years, Rootes and Standard both suffered from low productivity and sagging profits, being relegated to price takers rather than price leaders, so that it came as no surprise when eventually they were taken over by outside interests.[21]

It is hard to see what long-term benefits accrued from the Gang system and even at Standard it failed to live up to its promise. It did little to change workforce attitudes and within a short time even the hiring of labour came under a cloud, with rumours circulating that employment was often obtained unfairly. Black attempted to wrest this function away from the Gangs as early as 1950, but failed. Similarly, some of the Gangs constructed their own empires, sometimes engaging in bitter wrangling in order to secure lucrative new jobs. Attempts were made to deman Gangs in order to increase the earning power of the remaining members. A similar ploy involved the recruitment of an exceptionally large number of low rated workers which increased the share of the bonus going to those on higher rates. Ideally the system was meant to narrow differentials but this it patently did not do. As we have already seen, the degree of power devolved to the unions varied between firms, but regardless of this, and despite their accepted responsibilities, the unions for their part appear not to have developed a company or even plant wide view of industrial relations. Standard's TGWU-dominated Canley plant with 100 per cent union membership was the most tightly organised, but even this failed to prevent sectional squabbling or the firm's demise.

Rootes though appears to have suffered more than Standard from this syndrome with near continual inter-union feuding during the 1950s between the TGWU and the AEU over comparative rates of pay and rights of recruitment, all of which was exacerbated by pro and anti communist factionalism within the two unions. Indeed it is significant that from 1952 until 1960 there was no Joint Shop Stewards' Committee (JSSC) within the firm. Jaguar's position in the early 1960s also exhibited weaknesses at both union and management level in the conduct of industrial relations as is amply illustrated in Clack's study. He found that there was no senior personnel director and that the personnel manager was paid a lower salary than his status warranted. Major industrial relations problems were simply left as another part of the works manager's overall responsibilities. The stewards at Jaguar never enjoyed the quasi-managerial role of their counterparts at Standard, but Clack concluded that the general quality of union leadership was amateurish, with the JSSC having no coordinating role across the plant because of inter-union rivalries. The stewards, he argued, spent a great deal of time trying to nip disputes in the bud and preventing 'downers' and strikes in extremely difficult conditions.[22]

IV. The Move to Day-Work

Although there were no overt moves to break the power of the stewards until the mid-1960s, as early as 1954 Standard's management began to modify its approach towards labour relations. In that year Sir John Black was ousted in a boardroom coup led by Alick Dick, a fellow company director, who almost immediately began to assert greater managerial authority. A prominent TGWU convenor was sacked, attempts were made to prevent stewards from holding union meetings on the premises and stewards were also required to seek permission before holding Gang meetings and to disclose the content of these to the management. The laying off of 3,000 men, representing almost 40 per cent of the work force, during a period of recession in 1956 provided one important example of the new hard line approach. This occurred when Standard were in the course of installing new automatic transfer equipment and reflected Dick's policy of challenging union authority at a time when an increase in the capital–labour ratio strengthened the potential power of the shop-floor.

The shift in workplace policy associated with Dick was the beginning of what turned out to be a long term strategy designed to change the Gang and piecework systems as they operated in Coventry. Large Gangs were thought to be inflexible when technical change was required so that, for example, in planning the introduction of the Triumph Herald in the mid-1950s Dick introduced a larger number of smaller units in order to achieve greater mobility of labour. This process went ahead quite quickly and by 1960 there were again nearly a hundred Gangs in the Canley plant. Bold though this move in itself, it did little to erode the power of the stewards since in 1961 they were still able to force work-sharing during the downswing of that year when many other firms throughout the UK motor industry were shedding labour.[23]

Breaking up the Gangs was one thing, but to end piecework was a much riskier undertaking, liable to provoke labour unrest, particularly in the 1960s when the Coventry work force was becoming increasingly volatile as the industry stumbled and faltered. Cost-cutting in the assembly side of motor vehicle manufacture is never easy, especially in the short term, because of the heavy reliance upon outside suppliers. However, although labour represents a relatively small proportion of total costs, it is an area which traditionally management has targeted for economies. The piecework system exerted a ratchet effect on labour costs so that at Standard, for example, all new jobs negotiated between the stewards and the ratefixers had to yield a price not less than that paid for existing or previous jobs, and once Gang members had mastered the techniques of a new task it was easy to push up earnings. The importance of local bargaining is illustrated by the fact that between 1953 and 1969 it accounted for 72 per cent of all wage growth in Coventry, the remaining 28 per cent resulting for national agreements. The mid-1960s saw several inquiries into labour relations in the British motor industry, many of the most authoritative led by Jack Scamp. When concluding his investigation of labour disputes at Standard in 1966, Scamp identified the piecework system as the root cause, an opinion shared by the Rootes management in analysing its own poor industrial relations. Yet it must be stressed that wage drift was a problem throughout British industry and that the highest rates of increase were in shipbuilding and chemicals, while in Coventry the greatest culprits were Alvis and Bristol Siddeley, both of which were no longer concerned with the production of motor vehicles.

In this climate, the Coventry Toolroom Agreement became the focus of much debate. Although highly skilled, in many firms toolmen received a lower wage than some semi-skilled pieceworkers who were on the district skilled rate. Stress was placed less on the unfairness of the system, but rather on the way that the published toolroom rates became a rallying point for comparability as a pace setter for pieceworkers and were a more than useful bargaining weapon in wage negotiations. There were moves to abolish the Agreement in 1968 but employers recognised that as an average the toolroom rate avoided comparisons with peak figures and might well have played a role in moderating wage drift in the city. The Agreement was finally withdrawn in 1972 amid a general restructuring of wages in the industry and when the departure of BL from the CDEEA threatened to narrow significantly the base upon which rates were calculated. It seems highly probable that had the Agreement been abolished in the later 1960s, the stewards would have found some other yardstick against which to make comparisons.[24]

The conduct of labour relations in the motor industry generally, and in Coventry in particular, came under close scrutiny in the 1960s, especially with the establishment of the the Donovan Commission, and it was against this background that the main Coventry producers decided to end piecework and introduce Measured Day Work. Moreover, there had been major changes of ownership which greatly affected the autonomy of the Coventry firms. In 1967 Rootes relinquished control to the Chrysler Corporation, while Jaguar, which had earlier become part of BMH, was subsumed into BLMC in 1968. Such take-overs and mergers brought fundamental changes in managerial attitudes and decision making processes. The Coventry firms had simply become small scale operations in large national and multinational enterprises and their future would no longer be settled within the confines of the city. Rootes began the replacement of piecework with MDW in 1966, a policy subsequently endorsed by Chrysler, while BL moved in a similar direction in 1968 as part of a company wide wages reform package.[25]

Whatever justifications were used for the introduction of MDW in Coventry, there is little doubt that this was an attempt to reassert managerial control and bring an end to the Gang system. Following the appointment of Pat Lowry as Industrial Relations Director, BL made it clear that MDW was, in the company's view, the best way to organise a modern car plant. This arrangement was said to provide greater control over wage drift, eliminate continual bargaining, facilitate the more rapid introduction of technical change and encourage labour mobility without the need for protracted shop floor negotiation. MDW was intended to lead to greater output supervision, including track speed and loading levels, and provide scope for economies in clerical and administrative staff. The principal advantage to the work force was said to be less reliance on bonus payments which would help to minimise fluctuations in total earnings as well as reducing both sectional divisions between workers and inequalities in pay between direct and indirect workers.

In effect the companies were offering these benefits in return for the surrender of the principle of mutuality. When MDW was first suggested at Canley, Eddie McGarry, the influential Shop Stewards' Convenor, was quoted as saying 'We have decided that in no circumstances will we tolerate any interference with the present approach of payments by results or piecework systems unless the proposed changes are mutually agreed at domestic level'.[26] Despite protracted negotiations, the shop floor attitude had not changed by 1971 when senior shop stewards described the prospects of MDW as 'absolutely nil'.[27] The response at Jaguar was equally hostile and it was only after repeated strikes, including one of eleven weeks, that a settlement was eventually achieved with the new systems being introduced officially in 1974. The issue generated a similarly protracted struggle at Chrysler. When negotiations failed, the company announced that it would move unilaterally to MDW regardless of the union position. Attitudes quickly hardened with the workers voting against the company proposals and refusing to implement revised schedules. Chrysler eventually produced the incentive of an increased wage offer, placing its labour at the summit of Coventry earnings, and conceded slower track speeds than those currently in operation. The introduction of MDW proved to be no panacea. Both Chrysler and BL were ill prepared for it managerially with neither company having sufficient trained staff to police the shop floor. Of equal seriousness, Chrysler's industrial engineering department proved incapable of organising production efficiently to the extent that within a short period a form of mutuality was restored with the shop floor workers being left to establish their own pattern of work. Now that their power over rate and bonus bargaining had been ended, the stewards simply turned their attention from purely financial matters to issues concerned with status, pensions, holidays, safety and other fringe benefits. There was no significant improvement in labour relations, especially at Chrysler where some 500 strikes were recorded in the early 1970s. The company's labour relations policy was extremely confrontational and was all too often conducted by American managers with little knowledge of the subtleties of the British system and simply provoked a labour backlash at a time when it was blatantly obvious that the firm was in sharp decline and losing money heavily. Similarly, BL's problems, like those of Chrysler, were also far too serious to be solved by the erosion of the stewards' power by the removal of the Gang system.[28]

Although Chrysler and BL both succeeded in imposing MDW on their respective work forces, by 1975 neither appears to have gained much from the experience. Even allowing for their poor labour relations record, both firms were merely attacking the symptoms of decline rather than the root causes which were associated with the vicious circle of sagging profits, inadequate investment, poor model development and declining market share, all of which were ultimately the responsibility of management. In practice, MDW came too late to have any appreciable chance of arresting the pace of decline of either company. Chrysler's experience is particularly salutary. The firm persisted in pursuing its hard-line style of management down to 1975 by which time it was on the edge of bankruptcy and rumours of a pull-out by Detroit were rife. It was in the midst of this that in what seemed a last ditch attempt to solve the firm's appalling labour relations problems, exemplified by the 'electricians' staff status strike' and the 'shoddy work strike', the American parent ordered a softer approach to the unions. By this time both sides had begun to appreciate that communications and labour relations within the firm had to be improved and a series of joint union management committees were formed under the Employee Participation Programme to cover all aspects of plant organisation and policy. Although there is debate about the purity of the company's motives, there is little doubt that this represented a very public turnaround in its labour relations stance and, laudable though the objectives of participation were, they came too late to prevent the crisis of 1975 when the operation had to be baled out by the then Labour government to prevent a complete closure of Chrysler UK.[29]

So far as Coventry's BL plants are concerned, the introduction of MDW in 1974 had little impact on their long term future which was bound up with the company's wider problems and which culminated in partial public ownership. The stewards quickly relinquished their quasi-managerial functions, no longer bothering to book in work or chase up materials or parts, tasks which were left to the newly appointed supervisors. The new system is said to have reduced personal incentives in that however hard you worked the money remained the same. Increased labour manning on the tracks was welcomed as it reduced the physical stress, while a higher proportion of poor work was allowed to pass down the track as it no longer had any impact on wages.[30] Many have argued that in the short term MDW was strongly demotivating to the workers and perhaps this helps to explain why, when allied to job insecurity and closure threats, labour relations were so poor in Coventry's main car plants in the mid-1970s. MDW had failed to bring the stability its supporters sought.

V. Conclusion

Employer attitudes to labour relations in Coventry's motor industry from the Second World War until the mid-1970s were reactive rather than creative. Whenever difficulties arose or circumstances changed a short term solution was sought to what were essentially deeply entrenched problems, and in the long term little if anything was gained from such tactics. Before 1939 the motor industry was largely without trade union organisation. The war exacerbated labour market rigidities and this, together with the need to increase production quickly, provided the unions with the opportunity to establish a strong position within the car and aircraft plants. The readjustments of the immediate post-war years offered a similar mix of economic factors which allowed the unions to maintain their bargaining strength, despite futile attempts to dislodge them. The war had brought the recognition among employers that there was usually more to gain through cooperation than confrontation. Much has been written about the Coventry Gang system and the ceding of managerial prerogative to the shop stewards, thereby marginalising both regional and national union officials as well as foremen, but the degree to which this occurred varied between firms. Yet it was a management strategy which proved ephemeral, lasting only so long as the employers operated within a seller's market. The Gang system, with piecework as its mainspring, failed to launch the city's volume producers into the upper echelons of the 'Big Six'. Both Rootes and Standard remained small concerns with low profits, inadequate investment and a lagging market share with both firms ultimately welcoming take-over by healthier companies. Similarly, the system as it operated on the shop floor, did not of itself lead to more harmonious labour relations, as had been hoped. Inter-union and inter-Gang bickering continued with wage differentials being maintained or in many cases widened.

The honeymoon with the work force lasted in effect only until the early 1950s after which it was increasingly obvious that competition was becoming more forceful, especially in export markets, while at home Coventry's firms, with the exception of Jaguar, were diminishing in importance as motor vehicle producers within the UK. Yet to see the Gang system and piecework as the main causes of decline is to ignore the structural and managerial weaknesses within the main Coventry concerns. Though by the early 1960s the large Gangs were broken as part of the managerial drive to increase labour flexibility and achieve greater control over costs, management was not strong enough to mount a major frontal attack on piecework until near the end of the decade by which time both the volume producers had fallen into the arms of stronger companies. Even then the attempt to introduce MDW was successful but only after a long, hard and bitter struggle. MDW was seen as a panacea, but in the event it proved to be yet another short-term tactic which did little to halt the long decline of Coventry's motor industry.

NOTES

1. For an analysis of the development of the Coventry motor car industry during this period, see D. Thoms and T. Donnelly, *The Car Industry in Coventry Since the 1890s* (London, 1985).
2. Ibid., pp.85, 162.
3. W. Hornby, *Factories and Plant* (London, 1958), p.256.
4. J. Davy, *The Standard Car 1903–63* (Coventry, 1964), pp.40, 41.
5. A. Friedman, *Industry and Labour* (London, 1977), p.204.

6. S. Tolliday, 'Government, Employers and Shop Floor Organization in the British Motor Industry, 1939–69', in S. Tolliday and J. Zeitlin (eds.), *Shop Floor Bargaining and the State* (Cambridge, 1985), pp.109–17.
7. University of Warwick, Modern Records Centre, MSS. 180/MRB/3/3/21, 'Some Notes on the Characteristic Outlook and Attitude of Midlands Industry', p.2, 6 September 1945.
8. Public Records Office (PRO), CAB 102/406, Memorandum on Labour Welfare and Utilisation in the Aircraft Industry by J.B. Jeffreys, nd., p.50.
9. PRO, LAB 10/351, Midland Region, Weekly Report by the Industrial Relations Officer, 1 March 1941.
10. PRO, CAB 102.406, Memorandum on Labour Welfare, op. cit., Appendix B.
11. For Jones's own account of his work in Coventry at this time, see J. Jones, *Union Man* (London, 1986).
12. Thoms and Donnelly, op. cit., pp.146–147.
13. E. Wigham, *The Power to Manage* (London, 1973), pp.111–37.
14. Ibid., pp.146–7.
15. Ibid., pp.150–223.
16. W. Lewchuk, *American Technology and the British Motor Industry* (Cambridge, 1987), pp.196–9.
17. Ibid.
18. S. Tolliday, 'High Tide and After: Coventry Engineering Workers and Shop Floor Bargaining 1945–80' in W. Lancaster and T. Mason (eds.), *Life and Labour in a Twentieth Century City: The Experience of Coventry* (Coventry, 1986), pp.208–10.
19. K. Richardson, *Twentieth Century Coventry* (Coventry, 1972), p.119.
20. Tolliday, 'High Tide and After', op. cit., pp.215–210; S. Young and N. Hood, *Chrysler UK: A Corporation in Transition* (London, 1977), pp.210 et seq.
21. Friedman, op. cit., pp.210–21.
22. Tolliday, 'High Tide and After', op. cit., pp.219–24; see also G. Clack, *Industrial Relations in a British Car Factory* (Cambridge, 1967).
23. Thoms and Donnelly, op. cit., pp.166–8.
24. Tolliday, 'High Tide and After', op. cit., pp.234–5.
25. Young and Hood, op. cit., pp.224–231; A. Thornett, *From Militancy to Marxism* (London, 1987), pp.199–215.
26. *Coventry Evening Telegraph*, 23 Oct. 1968.
27. *Ibid.*, 14 Oct. 1971.
28. Thoms and Donnelly, op. cit., pp.206–7.
29. Young and Hood. op. cit., pp. 231–46.
30. Friedman, op. cit., pp.234–9.

INDEX

Tayleur, Charles, 9
Taylor, Frederick, 3
Taylorism, 32, 39, 43, 50–51
Thomas, J. H., 67–9, 74–5
Thoms, David, 6
Tilbury Docks, 52
Tolliday, S., 106
Transport & General Workers Union, 87,
    98, 107–8
Treasury Agreement (1915), 38
Triumph Herald, 108

Unemployment Insurance Act (1920), 59
Union of Women Matchmakers, 56
Ure, Andrew, 2–3

Vauxhall Motor Co., 106
Victoria & Albert Docks, 52
Vulcan Foundry, 9

Webb, F.W., 13–14, 20–21
Webb, Sidney & Beatrice, 2, 16
welfare measures, 5; railway
    workshops, 12–13; matchmaking,
    56–61; flour milling, 92, 94;
    motor vehicles, 105, 110
West Indies, 57
West Midlands, 101
Whitley Committee, 88

Zeitlin, Jonathan, 4, 9